HORSEBACK RIDING IN THE GREAT SMOKY MOUNTAINS NATIONAL PARK

Cades Cove Area

JODY L. BURRAGE

Published in the United States of America.

Cover Designer: Dana Leah, Designs by Dana
Editor: Lisa A. Hollett, Silently Correcting Your Grammar
Interior Layout: Deena Rae Schoenfeldt — E-Book Builders

Contents

HISTORICAL SIGNIFICANCE

On September 2, 1940, Franklin D. Roosevelt dedicated the Great Smoky Mountains National Park, "for the permanent enjoyment of the people," from the Rockefeller Memorial at Newfound Gap.

Unknown to some, FDR was a horseman like his distant cousin Teddy Roosevelt. Despite his physical condition later in life, FDR continued to ride horses along with his wife, Eleanor. He was an experienced horseman, and one of his famous quotes during World War II was, "you don't change horses midstream."

Mr. Roosevelt also took great interest in the environment, conservation, and forestry. Throughout his life, he considered himself a "tree farmer." Interestingly, his favorite tree was the tulip poplar, which thrives in the GSMNP. He enjoyed them so much that he planted a stand near his library at the Springwood family estate in Hyde Park, New York.

DEDICATION

This book is dedicated to my grandfather, Ralph Samuel Patterson, whose love for the wilderness and mountains greatly influenced me. My earliest memories are sitting upon his shoulders, venturing into the surrounding valleys and mountains near our home. While growing up, I spent many a day hunting for arrowheads and ginseng, fishing, and exploring those same mountains and valleys by his side. As we journeyed along, he often shared stories of old ways forgotten. Among those stories, he spoke of a smooth Tennessee Walking Horse he owned named Betty. He also shared stories of his grandfather, Reno Patterson, who delivered mail via horseback in the Appalachian Mountains of North Carolina.

Today, when I step into any wilderness, my grandfather's gentle spirit endures within me. I can hear his kind voice speaking of pleasant things, times we shared together, and guiding me as he would have liked venturing along in the forest.

SYNOPSIS

The Great Smoky Mountains National Park is world-renowned for its diverse forests. Within its beautiful range, there are 550 miles of trails for equestrians to explore. Cades Cove is one of the most popular and scenic regions, and you can explore its backcountry on horseback.

Horseback Riding in the Great Smoky Mountains provides equestrians a detailed description of the horse trails found in the Cades Cove area. The safety of both the rider and the horse is of utmost importance, as are trail and land preservation. The unique dual difficulty ratings found exclusively in this guide will help you decide which trails are best suited for you and your horse.

Additional information within this one-of-a-kind guide also covers many other helpful topics, such as how to monitor horse vital signs, first aid, pre-ride checklists, equipment, trail preservation tips, park donations, and local emergency contacts. You'll also find trail pictures, locations of equestrian camping areas, and where to locate boarding facilities near Cades Cove. Equipped with this information, you'll be prepared for the trip before ever leaving home.

Experience the Smoky Mountains in a way most visitors never do—from the front-row seat atop your trusty steed in the most visited national park in the country.

ACKNOWLEDGMENTS

Special thanks to Melody Gilbertson, the owner of Lazy Horse Retreat, who provided the cabins and stables where I stayed while creating this guidebook. Her friendly nature always remained welcoming while answering my thousand questions and phone calls.

Thanks to Sam Berg, a hiker I met out on the trail who was kind enough to befriend me and send me information on the Great Smoky Mountains National Park. Her insights were valuable concerning trail usage from a hiker's point of view.

Head Backcountry Ranger Christina Hoyer for answering my many emails and questions about the Smoky Mountain Backcountry.

Great Smoky Mountains Association Retail Director Dawn Roark for responding to my emails and questions.

The backcountry rangers who were always courteous and helpful every time I called with questions. You provide a valuable service to the many visitors who come to enjoy the park.

Friends of the Smokies CEO Tim Chandler for helping to create the Leave No Trace Equestrian Fund to receive donations for preserving the horse trails of the Smokies.

All my horse friends who supported me, and the friendly people out on the trails I encountered. A special thank you to the hiker who unknowingly provided the picture for the cover of this book at Gregory Bald.

FOREWORD

*H*orseback Riding in the Great Smoky Mountains is the first book in a series covering the different horse areas within the park. This book was written to help horseback riders explore the Cades Cove area safely and with few hindrances. Unlike studying brochures and maps, the information in this book will help you better prepare before leaving home on your journey. Not only does it illustrate the trails more thoroughly, but it will inform you on many other details not well-known to visitors. In addition to more information on the trails, other topics have been added to enrich your pleasure and knowledge.

Horse trail preservation is actively encouraged throughout the text for both the present and the future generations to come. Moreover, this book serves as a constant proponent for preserving horseback riding. Unlike other national parks, the GSMNP operates partially on donations because it doesn't charge admission fees. While setting out to create this horse guide, it was my goal also to create a horse trail donation fund to support riding opportunities. By partnering with the Friends of the Smokies, I was able to make that hope come true. You can become a part of preserving this beautiful wilderness for future equestrians by donating. Be sure to review the *Preservation for the Great Smoky Mountains Horse Trails* page near the end of this book to learn how and where to send your donations.

Many tourists who venture here often forget, or do not know, that horses and mules played a significant role in helping the settlers who forged a living among the hills and valleys. Along with those early settlers, Native Americans also utilized horses extensively. The Cherokee were avid horse traders and excellent horsemen. Their training ability and breeding practices produced high-quality animals which were often passed down with great pride from father to son. Their horses were first acquired from Spanish missions across the deep South and then west of Mississippi during the early colonial days. As American natives became more adept at horse breeding, tribal horses gained quite a reputation for being excellent specimens, as noted in historical journals. Cherokee-bred horses were usually flashy Paints with gaited genetics.

Horses, mules, and donkeys helped forge our roads, plow our fields, carry our belongings, fight our wars, and discover new lands throughout the ages. Those were not the only capacities in which they served humankind. They are responsible for creating entertainment, jobs, and even to help rehabilitate people with crippling disorders. You see, without our four-legged companions, many of the accomplishments and advancements we enjoy in modern times could not have occurred.

Simply stated, our world is much more vibrant because of them.

A chapter near the end of this book, *History of Man and Equine*, provides a brief historical account of how society and horses evolved alongside each other. I believe you will find it fascinating because it describes how primitive cultures first utilized equines. Much of what the ancient civilizations learned led to the creation of the many trades and developments we employ in the horse industry today.

Lastly, with every word in this guide, I've shared my deep admiration for horses and the wilderness, and I hope it inspires you to feel the same. I cannot think of any animal in creation that's so noble or revered with which to spend time in the Great Smoky Mountains. It is my sincere hope you explore all the trails safely at Cades Cove, as each one will leave an indelible memory to cherish for a lifetime.

By virtue, Equines have served humans in roles that have been vital to the advancement of both civilizations and their pleasure. As such, riders and their steeds have every right to enjoy the park's many designated trails. That is, after all, part of the park's heritage.

Sincerely,

Jody L. Burrage

Enjoying a high mountain cliff ride on a flashy gaited Paint.

INTRODUCTION

Scores of delightful books have been written about the Great Smoky Mountains, covering a wide variety of topics. However, a well-thought-out horse guide had yet to be written for those who long to experience the rugged trails within this southeastern national park. Until now.

Sure, there are maps and brochures located within the park that are specific to horse camping and the trails. You can even download information from the park's website or other web portals. The problem is, it's just enough info to temporarily lull you into thinking you won't encounter any problems on your journey.

Don't get me wrong—the park works hard to provide visitors with necessary information. They even have rangers available to discuss backcountry activities with you on the phone seven days a week. Indeed, they receive high marks for all they do. You'd think, with all these available resources, it would make for an always successful and safe trip to Cades Cove with your horse. But that just isn't the case, since horseback riders need more information beforehand than the typical visitor. It's not as simple as strapping on your hiking boots and throwing your backpack in the car before hitting the trail. There's a lot more to consider and plan for because something forgotten or unknown can easily ruin the costly trip.

For starters, having a thorough knowledge of the area roads is essential before hauling your thousand-pound horse to the desired trailhead inside the park. The path you need to travel may not accommodate your trailer. Parking areas and peak tourist seasons are but a couple of the other crucial aspects to consider. Most importantly, horseback riders should be acutely aware of the trail's potential dangers and required skill level to make informed decisions before venturing into a remote wilderness area.

You may ask what qualifies me to write this book and provide my insights on the topics contained within these pages. That is a fair question, and I'll gladly share my experience with you. Foremost, I'm a rugged outdoorsman and skilled horseman who has made numerous rescues in wilderness settings for trauma and medical patients. In addition to spending more hours in the woods than in my home—be it hiking, hunting, camping, or riding horses—I'm a blacksmith, farrier, and the author of another horse trail guidebook covering the northwest Georgia area. While serving as a member of the Backcountry Horsemen Association of Northwest Georgia, I became versed in trail maintenance and land preservation. Lastly, I'm a descendant of cavalrymen and horsemen on multiple sides of my family—guess you could say it's in my DNA. To my knowledge, the GSMNP hasn't had an individual with my desire, passion, and aptitude write a horse trail book to help horsemen navigate the park.

Consequently, this book was born out of necessity. The first time I visited Cades Cove with my horse, I was more than frustrated to have gone through the chore of gathering all my gear and hauling my animals from two hours away, only to find I couldn't ride the trail as planned. One vital detail I quickly learned was that my large horse trailer prevented me from accessing the trails located on the narrow one-way park roads around the Cove. Additionally, it was extremely challenging to turn around or get help, and there is no cell service in that area to contact park officials to advise me of further options.

While encountering bumper-to-bumper traffic filled with sight-seeing tourists, I realized most people don't understand the complexities involved in towing a large rig with horses onboard in the most visited area of the Smokies. Also, tiny parking lots blocked by those same tourists can lead to more problems—or an abrupt end to your journey.

Like all national parks, there are some genuine safety concerns and dangers. You know, the things no one bothered to tell you about and you only discover when you're on a horse and faced with the dilemma firsthand. But hey, not every danger can be mentioned because, off the main road, this is still considered an untamed wilderness. Sometimes, park officials have a difficult time properly advising riders across a wide range of experience levels while simultaneously maintaining the integrity of the wilderness.

So, without pressing my point further on problematic encounters, this guide is designed to increase your knowledge instead of your having to piece information together from various sources. Or worse, having to visit multiple times before you figure out the "ins and outs" around the Cove. It will help you better plan and prepare before beginning your trip to its rugged interior. I have assembled well-thought-out, need-to-know information, with your safety and that of your horse in mind, to make your journey as trouble-free as possible. Extras are included for your enjoyment too. All this from a die-hard horse enthusiast who takes horseback riding seriously.

Having enlightened you as to the inception of this book, let's press forward to see what this national park offers.

The GSMNP has an astounding 500 plus miles of horse trails spanning the entire region, with a broad array of terrain to explore. But have you ever read what you will experience on those trails? If not, you're in for one fun and fantastic adventure—one you'll not soon forget. Stand in awe of the many waterfalls and streams flowing from the mountain heights or through the valleys. Fill your soul with views from one of its spruce-fir high-altitude forests. Whether you arrive during the verdant, green days of spring and summer or the brilliance of fall's changing colors, you'll find an enticing forest vista around every turn. When you venture into one of the world's few remaining Biosphere Reserves, unique varieties of plants, animals, and pristine forests will captivate your heart.

While the park's natural charm entices visitors, history reveals that early settlers, mounted upon their steeds, explored some of the park's most famous locations. One such site is Clingmans Dome, formerly known as Kuwa'hi by the Cherokee. This renowned mountain peak was later renamed after Thomas Clingman, who forged trails through the dense forests on horseback to survey the land in the early 1850s. Still, there were settlers plowing fields to feed their families, while others cut roads and cleared land as small villages prospered, all using horse and mule power.

Raids by mounted cavalrymen during the American Civil War enrich the park's equestrian history further. The entire region was traversed by horses and mules for many reasons over the years of its occupancy. Two notable horsemen found in the park's history annals are John W. Oliver, who delivered mail via horseback in Cades Cove and John W. Ogle, who resided in Pigeon Forge and served his community as a doctor, reaching patients by his trusted horse. Indeed, there are many other accounts of horsemen found within these hills and valleys which would create a fascinating book.

Visitors often take for granted the contributions equine made to the region. Some of the routes in the park, used by millions of visitors today, were created by these hard-working animals. Also, they helped create a life for early residents long before this area became a national playground, with its numerous hiking trails and pull-offs.

Famous settlers are often remembered, and locations were named after them. But it was only because of horse and mules that men made great strides for their communities in these rugged mountains. For that reason alone, horses and mules are as much of an integral part of the park's history as any human being. Even today, horses are utilized in trail maintenance by volunteers and park rangers. Horses can also be used during emergencies on trails where all-terrain vehicles cannot tread.

Of course, as any true horseman knows, the best way to explore a landscape worth venturing is on the back of a cherished steed. Why? Because the horse provides a front-row seat to a most brilliant theater not made by human hands. Likewise, bonding with our beloved ground-thumpers in a beautiful wilderness makes for the best adventure a person could desire in life.

So, let's begin. I hope you enjoy this one-of-a-kind guide crafted just for horse folks in the Great Smoky Mountains at Cades Cove.

Happy trails.

PHYSIOGRAPHIC REGION

At roughly 800 square miles, this landmass comprises the largest protected wilderness east of the Rocky Mountains. It is further surrounded by over 1.5 million acres of national forestland, providing rows of mountains, ridges, and valleys with sweeping panoramic views.

Currently the most visited national park in North America, the GSMNP is situated at the southern end of the oldest mountain range in the world, the Appalachians. This well-known mountain range in the southeastern US stretches from Georgia to Maine and is home to the longest hiking trail in the world at 2,200 miles long. It is known as the Appalachian National Scenic Trail.

Interestingly, this diverse collection of mountain peaks, valleys, and rivers is a subrange of the Blue Ridge Mountain Physiographic Province. Its boundaries are found within Tennessee and North Carolina. Elevations range from 875 to 6,643 feet, with sixteen peaks rising more than 5,000 feet within the park. Monte Le Conte is the tallest mountain from base to top, peaking at 6,593 feet, and Clingmans Dome has the highest peak above sea level at 6,643 feet.

The park is estimated to contain 187,000 acres of old-growth forest and is designated as a United Nations World Heritage Site and International Biosphere Reserve. There are five forest types found within the Smokies. Each forest system is unique in its own composition, location, and structure.

Knowing how to identify each forest type will enrich your experience significantly. You may even want to obtain a book for further study on the subject, which can be found at one of the five visitor centers within the park.

The hallmark of the Smoky Mountains is its diverse forest types. The diversity is determined by exposure, elevation, and moisture.

Spruce-Fir Forest (Highest Elevations)

The red spruce and Fraser fir trees can be found thriving above 4,500 feet elevation in what is known as the Southern Appalachian Spruce-Fir forest. This beautiful ecoregion is roughly 100 square miles in size and resembles the Boreal forests of Canada, but is unique unto itself. It is among the highest and coldest climates found within the southern Appalachian range. Temperatures can reach as low as -30°F in the winter, with winds causing much harsher conditions. Snowfall is estimated to be around sixty-nine inches at Newfound Gap, which has an elevation of 5,046 feet.

During the summer months, heavy rainfall drenches these higher elevations more so than the valleys, producing the many waterfalls cascading down the slopes. The runoff then forms larger tributaries, such as streams and rivers found down below. High winds and thunderstorms are not uncommon.

Much of the time, the spruce-fir forest is draped in dense clouds, keeping the forest continually moist. This wet, herbaceous floor is covered with many shade-tolerant ferns. There are over seventy different varieties. Several hundred species of thick mosses also grow prolifically. On the forest floor, understory plants are very abundant. Mountain ash, pin cherry, and Catawba rhododendron are among some of the many species found. Of course, many species of beautiful flowers also thrive at these elevations too.

It is estimated that 85% of the southern spruce-fir forest lies within the national park, Blue Ridge Parkway, and other nearby state-owned lands. Currently, this one-of-a-kind ecosystem is classified as an endangered region. The causes behind this classification are the result of different reasons, such as invasive insects and pollution. However, many studies are underway which are focused on ways to preserve it.

Pine-Oak Forest (Below 4000 feet)

The hottest and driest forest areas are made up of xerophytic pines and oaks found on south-facing slopes throughout the park. The pines dominate on open ridges while the oak trees grow in moister soil. A bright climate produces tangles of mountain laurel and huckleberry under the open canopy while the herbaceous floor layer produces, wintergreen, and trailing arbutus. Timber rattlesnakes are often encountered sunning on the rocky outcroppings. Large colonies of the herb Galax grow abundantly, and the most common wildflower is the orchid species, although other brilliant types can be seen.

Many of the park's boundary trails pass through these desiccant ranges when they crest ridges and curve around to the south side of the mountains. These hot and arid areas contrast significantly with the other forest types found within the park and are at a higher risk for fire.

Eastern Hemlock Forest (1500 – 4500 feet)

This forest is distinguished by the dominance of a deep green conifer tree—the Eastern Hemlock. Found on slopes, ridges, flats, and stream corridors throughout the park. These areas are usually shady, moist, and produce a thick, springy mat of needles on the ground underneath. Most trees, with their massive trunks, stand 100 feet and give a beautiful cathedral effect to the surrounding forest. Many water tributaries are commonly found nearby the stands of Hemlocks, adding to the overall charm and producing some of the most beautiful spots in the park.

Although the Hemlock tree dominates these spaces, other tree species are sometimes mingled-in, such as the Frasier Magnolia, the Silverbell, and Yellow Birch. Understory plants consist of American Holly, Striped Maple, and Black Birch.

Many species of animals use the Hemlock forests for primary habitat, but over the last few years, the forest has come under attack by the wooly adelgid. These non-native insects threaten the forests by killing the trees, thereby resulting in a significant change to the ecosystem. Many conservation efforts are underway to preserve these areas.

Northern Hardwood Forest (High Mountain Slopes)

Elevations between 4,000-5,500 feet on the high mountain slopes form this beautiful zone. There are more tree species found within this section of the park than there are tree species found in all of Europe. It also has the highest concentration of broadleaf tree species in the eastern United States and provides the most picturesque views during the fall.

A few tree types found within this section are the northern red oak, sugar maple, yellow birch, American beech, and fire cherry. Magnificent displays of these trees and many more can be viewed along the abundant pull-offs while trailering to the park.

If you glance upward, the mountain will reveal the merging of the northern hardwoods into the spruce-fir zone, called the ecotone. Noticeably, the tall, conical shape of the red spruce tree will stand out among the upper northern hardwoods where they merge.

Cove Hardwood Forest

Cove hardwood forests are found in protected valleys and on northern-facing slopes from the lowest elevations up to 4,500 feet. Upon entering this forest, the open-gallery appearance of this forest reveals large towering tulip trees, basswood, and yellow buckeye trees. Their rich, leafy canopies reach heights over 150 feet. Trunk diameters often reach four feet in diameter in the second growth portions. The old-growth areas can produce tree trunks in widths of six feet.

The undergrowth of the cove hardwood forest contains many species of shrubs, flowers, and vines, but they are not as prolific as in the other forest areas. The lack of ground cover in this area makes the forest appear more open, revealing the towering trees. Some of the shrub species are the flowering dogwood, Catawba rhododendron, mountain laurel, and the smooth hydrangea. Deep, fertile, moist soils found in these areas support the abundant tree and plant life.

Tulip popular trees are commonly found throughout the Smoky Mountains with four-to-five-foot trunk diameters.

All horses within the park should be on a highline when taking a break or camping.

Wild Flowers and Shrubs

There are more than 1,400 wild flower species found within the park from the valley to the peak. Among some of the notable species often seen are trilliums, Solomon's seal, Dragon's Advocate, orchids, bee balm, and Dutchman's breeches.

Perhaps the most unusual plants in the park that catch visitors' attention are the nine species of flowering shrubs. Usually displaying a dazzling show of colors, these shrubs are the rhododendrons and azaleas. At the middle altitudes, thriving around shadowy ravines and streams, are the rosebay rhododendrons. They bloom between June and August with white flowers.

Wild azalea blooming in late May.

Bee balm in July.

Catawba rhododendrons are at higher elevations, often found where trees do not grow. These shrublands, called heath balds, produce purple flowers which can cover large ridge faces. They bloom between May and June. Unlike the others, flame azaleas grow at nearly all elevations and bloom at different intervals, depending upon the altitude at which they are found. Their colors range from white, peach, orange, yellow to red. Flowers start blooming in April at low elevations and progress through June to the higher elevations.

Along the trails and roadways, mountain laurel can be seen blooming with pink or white flowers May through June. These laurel patches are often referred to as laurel slicks.

Mountain laurel blooming during early June.

Tributaries

Due to the park's geographic location, abundant warm air from the Gulf of Mexico and the Atlantic Ocean cools as it rises over the mountains. This cooling effect causes increasing amounts of precipitation at the higher elevations, thus creating numerous cascades and waterfalls throughout the entire range.

As the water flows steadily down the steep mile-high summits, it forms streams, creeks, and rivers. There are many famous waterfalls found within the park, and some of the rivers can be enjoyed for leisure. Because of the abundant moisture, amphibians thrive in the Smoky Mountains, and the park is known as the Salamander Capital of the World.

Weather

The park's weather pattern can be summed up as having four distinct seasons. Temperatures during any season are different at the higher elevations, around 5,000 to 6,600 feet. Mountain weather can also be unpredictable, so be prepared when venturing out on trails at these altitudes. It is not uncommon to experience a temperature difference of twenty degrees with high winds. Also, clouds bearing rain or snow can occur rapidly depending on the time of year. Below is a brief summation of the seasons.

Summer produces typical southern weather at the lower elevations—hot and humid with frequent thunderstorms. While at higher elevations, the temperature is pleasantly warm. Hazy days are common.

Fall produces cooler days and nights with less rain in the mountains. The lack of moisture and falling thermometer mean reduced haze, bringing about clearer skies and revealing the colorful images of the landscape with the season changes. Higher elevations can produce freezing temperatures and snowfall during the late fall months.

Winter weather is usually mild in the valleys, with above-freezing days and colder nights. Temperatures at the high peaks are subfreezing with frequent snow accumulation. It's not uncommon to reach below zero for extended periods at higher elevations.

Spring brings about the most unpredictable weather patterns. Temperatures fluctuate from freezing to warm and rain to snow without much warning. The elevation dictates the severity of the weather. During this time of year, anyone out on the trails should be well prepared with multiple types of clothing garments for layering.

Wildlife

The most abundant wildlife in the Great Smoky Mountains includes deer, raccoons, turkey, elk, coyotes, and bobcats. But perhaps the most popular animal is the American black bear. A long-standing symbol of the park, black bears roam freely in the most extensive protected habitat of the southeast.

A lesser-known icon of the park is the salamander. This wilderness has been titled the Salamander Capital of the World because of the many different species found within its streams and wet areas.

All in all, the park supports sixty-five species of mammals, around sixty-seven species of fish, and more than 200 varieties of birds. Amphibians and reptiles number over eighty different types. Among the most popular places to view these animals are Cades Cove, Cataloochee Valley, and the Roaring Fork Motor Trail.

Panther Creek in the fall.

Deer grazing in early spring in Cades Cove.

American black bear commonly found in Cades Cove.

LOW-IMPACT RIDING

Before modern times, people had better horse-sense because horses were utilized every day. People were conscious of the dangers horses could inflict upon humans by merely being near them continually. In today's world, it's no different in our awareness of motor vehicles. We know the inherent risks and dangers of being too close while a car is in operation, so we take the necessary precautions to avoid accidents. But our modern times have caused horsemanship to be largely forgotten by many.

Cades Cove is the most popular attraction in the Great Smoky Mountains. It draws many campers, sightseers, hikers, and photographers. Heavy encounters with these visitors should be expected on the roads and parking areas before reaching the solitude of the rugged trails. But do not let them discourage you from the experience. The ride is well worth it.

Managing your horse around these curious visitors is crucial. It requires you to be conscientious and attentive to potential dangers because they simply don't understand horses. Moreover, it's equally important how you communicate with them during these interactions. If you come across as arrogant, loud, or condescending, scolding them about horse dangers, you will most likely leave a lasting adverse impression. This will reflect poorly on all horseback riders in the park and create negative feelings that will ultimately get reported to park rangers. The result is that it negatively impacts the future of horseback riding in the Great Smoky Mountains.

As a responsible horseman, you are an ambassador for the future preservation of our beloved animals and riding opportunities. So, help someone else out on the trail if the need arises, and always maintain a positive image. Preserve the wilderness and reflect positively upon this practice we call horsemanship. Additionally, as a "guest of the forest," it is your responsibility to leave it as you found it. Allow those following in your footsteps to enjoy the wilderness as you have.

The following guidelines can help ensure horseback riding will continue to be allowed in the future and make for an enjoyable experience for all who come to this great park.

Leave No Trace

Stay on the trails. Horses leave footprints and displace ground; therefore, stay on designated paths to preserve the natural habitat. Sometimes the trail is blocked by a fallen tree or landslide. If you encounter a blocked trail, refrain from going around if the alternative path causes damage or is unsafe. Report the issue to the backcountry office promptly at 865-436-1297. Carrying a saw or an ax can remedy many of these obstacles and help you finish the ride.

Respect others on the trail. Hikers are expected to yield when horses are passing for the safety of all parties. This is commonly known trail etiquette, but it is not always practiced. Whichever occurs, be courteous and conscientious when passing to avoid leaving a poor impression by your actions or remarks. Adverse reports to park officials concerning horseback riders can cause negative feelings about future horse use. Be an advocate for horsemen by connecting positively with others using the trail. If this goal cannot be achieved, move on safely and quietly.

Pack it in, pack it out. Nothing can be more irritating and frustrating than finding garbage within a pristine forest. Litter, in even the smallest form, always leaves a negative feeling with the others who use and enjoy the trails responsibly. Garbage and clutter scattered on the forest floor can also ruin someone else's experience. Go a step further— if you see a bit of litter on the trail, pick it up and pack it out.

Latrine Use. If the urge to relieve yourself cannot wait while you're deep in the forest, move off the trail or campsite and well away from water sources. Dig a six-inch hole and cover up your business. Not doing so is a health hazard, not to mention a disgusting sight.

Feeding or Approaching Wildlife. Animals of the park are wild. They are not pets and can inflict harm, and some can even endanger your life. Feeding, approaching, or pushing them all have negative consequences for both you and the animal. So, why would you jeopardize the animal's life or your own? Admire wildlife from a distance and do no harm. Besides, it's illegal, and others who see you do it will report you to park authorities.

Obeying the Rules. You will find many rules and policies regarding horseback riding and camping at Cades Cove. Following them is always the best practice. Be diligent in making yourself aware of them to avoid fines or citations.

RIDER EQUIPMENT AND SAFETY

Preparations

Before embarking on any horseback adventure in the park, always tell someone where you will be traveling and your estimated time of return. Taking another rider along with you will provide an extra measure of safety in case of an unlikely accident. Plan your ride well, and always have a safety plan.

First Aid

Traveling into the wilderness requires one to be conscientious of all dangers which could arise suddenly upon your horse. If you plan on spending any significant amount of time in the forest interior, it makes sense to complete a first aid course. If that isn't an option, carry a first aid kit. In addition to the kit, take a pocket first aid manual and learn to use it. It may save your or your friend's life.

In the event of someone becoming injured, first protect yourself and don't become a victim. Then, try to help the person without risking further injury. If this cannot be achieved, provide comfort and warmth, and reassure the victim that you will return with help. Leave needed things which may help the victim, and mark the exact location well before going to get help. First, you should assess the person's condition and form a general impression of the overall seriousness. Next, make a note of all the wounds, especially the details of the injured person's chief complaint. Lastly, if you're trained in basic first aid, take the victim's vital signs and write them down, along with the current time. You should also time yourself walking out to provide to rescue personnel.

Always tell someone where you will be and when to expect you back. If you're injured while riding alone, your best chance for help will come from how well you communicated where you were going and when you'll return. Perhaps another trail user may come by and render aid, but this can't be relied upon. Failure to tell someone your plans while venturing alone in the wilderness, only to then have a life-threatening accident, is a terrible way to succumb to death.

> *The most serious dangers to horseback riders include head trauma, falls, heat or cold exposure, venomous animals, or stinging insects.*

Rider Safety Equipment

Some equestrians do not wear safety gear while riding, but statistics show that head injuries are the most commonly sustained life-threatening injury. Those injuries are usually caused by unforeseen events while riding your horse, but surprisingly, a percentage occur by just being around them. Equestrian groups such as the Equestrian Medical Safety Association (EMSA) have studied the risks and found that head injuries related to riding horses outnumber football, bicycle, and motorcycle accidents. So, many head injuries can be prevented by wearing an American Society for Testing and Materials (ASTM) and Safety Equipment Institute (SEI) certified helmet.

Aside from head injuries, broken bones, cuts, bruises, and scrapes can occur. Chafing is a prevalent nuisance but can be prevented by wearing appropriate clothing. There are numerous types of garments and gear available to help protect yourself.

Consider the following suggestions:

- **Boots**: footwear specifically made for riding protect the feet, ankle, and allow for easy removal from the stirrups. Knee-high boots protect the shin and calf.

- Pants: heavy cotton, compression, leather, or stretch-type pants can help keep you comfortable.

- Legs: chinks or half-chaps can protect against lacerations, punctures, or abrasions.

- Torso: body protectors offer a degree of protection from impacts suffered from horse-related activities.

- Gloves: leather gloves protect the hands from abrasions, punctures, cuts, and scrapes.

- Outer Wear: rain garments, dusters, and wide brim hats help protect you from the elements.

Temporarily Lost

Using a map and this trail guide will almost always prevent you from getting turned around, but it can still occur. If you find yourself in this situation, stay calm and try to retrace your path on the map first. Do not leave the trail. Usually, you will determine your error and make corrections. If not, you may have to settle down for the night and begin at daylight because of lost time. Traveling at night will only cause more confusion and can be treacherous in unknown territory.

Here are a few pointers:

- 🐎 Tell someone your riding route ahead of time.

- 🐎 Your cell phone may pick up a signal at higher elevations.

- 🐎 Listen for sounds that indicate other people are around. There may be other trail users nearby to offer help.

If you followed the advice from the park's literature and this book, someone should come looking for you during a long period away. Again, taking a compass, map, and this book will help you immensely if you lose your way.

Conditioning

Riding stresses ankles, knees, rubs thighs, and strains your back. It also sores the hind-end, so you'll need to shape up before taking long rides into the mountains. Taking frequent short trips beforehand helps to ward off many of these problems. Exercising will condition your body and will also help you understand the load your horse is under while working.

Hiking on trails similar to the rugged terrain in which you plan to ride is an excellent way to become fit for such an adventure. Strap a weighted pack on your back for added measure. This accomplishes several things, such as strengthening your legs and back, while taxing the cardiovascular system. It also gives you an idea of what stressors your horse will be under and teaches you to pace yourself. Thus, riding your horse will be no different because you will be pacing him throughout his work efforts.

Steep Grades

Consideration must be given to the constant elevation changes within the park. Under the best-case scenario, your horse will provide your transportation for the entire trail. But if your horse becomes injured, there's a possibility you will have to walk him for several miles. Pay attention to your horse for signs of overexertion and stay well within your and the horse's capabilities.

Plan your ride accordingly using this guide, along with other trusted sources. That will give you a better understanding of the obstacles and terrain. Do not attempt rides longer than you can accomplish in daylight hours, or take unnecessary risks. You will always enjoy your trip more if you and the horse are in reasonably good shape.

Hypothermia

Hypothermia is the number one killer when it comes to outdoor trauma and can be a danger even in the warmer months. Clothing preparations must be carefully considered because temperatures can vary from peak to valley as much as ten to twenty-five degrees in the park. Subjection to sudden rain, wind, drop in temperature, or immersion in cold water begins the process of hypothermia. Extra layers, thermals, and waterproof clothing are a must even when you don't think they are necessary. Serious injuries increase the risk of hypothermia exponentially.

Drinking from Streams

The risk of giardiasis is high, as it's the most common waterborne disease in the southeastern United States. It is often referred to as beaver fever. Symptoms include abdominal pain and cramping, bloating, flatulence, and watery diarrhea. It is spread by the parasite colonizing in the upper small intestine.

Cysts containing dormant giardia are passed in the stools of animals into water sources. Beavers, otters, raccoons, deer, bear, and other mammals are among the list spreading the parasite. Even humans can spread it. Hence, it is not safe to drink water from streams, no matter how remote they are or how clean and pure they seem to be.

Safe water is boiled or treated with Globaline. Potassium iodide can also be used. Commercial grade water filters can safely screen the parasite out of water for consumption too.

Horse Conditioning, Equipment, and Safety

To help protect against injuries, horses need conditioning too. Those in average shape can usually handle a three- or four-hour trail ride on the weekends without much stress. But if you'll be taking longer trips in the mountains, you'll have to condition your horse to inclines, walking on rocks, and other challenging terrains.

A horse that previously hasn't been trained or conditioned to perform as required simply doesn't hold up to riding long distances on rugged mountain trails. Not only physical conditioning is needed, but acclimating your horse to its harnessed tack while under load is essential. Too many riders assume their horses are automatically up to the task, then cause their horse unnecessary injuries or pain with ill-fitted tack on difficult trails.

Conditioning your horse by spending increasingly extended periods under saddle on terrain similar to which you plan to ride is an excellent method to follow. The weight-bearing conditioning also improves your horse's balance and stamina while enabling him to get in shape much more quickly than round-pen exercises.

Tack

Proper, well-fitting equipment (tack) is essential to you and your horse since he is the one bearing the load for long distances in diverse terrain. I've always said a comfortable horse is a safer horse. The fact is, many serious problems can occur if certain tack items were to break or pressure points begin to irritate the horse beyond its pain threshold.

So, inspecting tack often for wear or damage can save you from unexpected incidents. Check your horse regularly for those pressure points. Many times, the culprit of an unruly horse is ill-fitting tack causing pain.

Well-fitted saddle and tack are essential.

A comfortable trail saddle adequately fitted to the horse's back, with a high-quality wool or felt saddle pad, is vitally important. The proper fit provides comfort for both the horse and rider on long mountain rides. Securing the saddle with a nonslip main and rear girth also is needed when riding in gradient terrain. A breast collar is added for more support, keeping the saddle from sliding rearward on steep inclines. It also serves as a safety in case the main girth belt breaks. In such an event, the saddle may roll sideways but will not come off. Sometimes, a crupper, secured around the tail and to back of the saddle, is used to stop the saddle from sliding forward; however, it is not needed if the saddle is correctly fitted. On slab-sided (less round barrel) horses and mules, full-breeching tack is the best harnessing system to use in the mountains. It will keep the saddle from sliding forward or rearward.

Good quality saddlebags with padding on the underside will carry both your food and gear without chafing your horse. Cantle bags are suitable for small items or stuffing a jacket inside. There are many variations of horn and pommel bags on the market to complete your setup. Ride often to build your perfect rig. The list below will help you get started.

⋔ Ax or Saw	⋔ Bug repellent	⋔ Trail Marker Tape
⋔ Map	⋔ Compass	
⋔ Cord	⋔ Duct Tape	⋔ First aid kits
⋔ Gloves	⋔ Headlamp	⋔ Multi-tool
⋔ Lariat	⋔ Lead rope	⋔ Collapsible Cup
⋔ Hobbles	⋔ Rain poncho	
⋔ Zip ties		⋔ Extra Clothes

First Aid for Horse

This list is meant to be a starting point. Consider adding additional items for your horse's specific needs.

⋔ Vaseline or Desitin	⋔ Wound Disinfectant	⋔ Tape
⋔ Self-adhesive leg wrap	⋔ Sterile gauze and bandage	⋔ Thermometer
⋔ Electrolyte supplement	⋔ Phenylbutazone (NSAID) pain	⋔ Banamine (NSAID) pain

Signs of an Exhausted and Dehydrated Horse

In the early stages of exhaustion, the horse will be depressed, have little interest in his surroundings, and will not respond well to cues. He will lack energy, occasionally tripping or stumbling. Heavy sweating will appear. Usually, the horse has no appetite and may not drink even when he is dehydrated. The eyes may be dull, and he may have a sagging lower lip, ears, and head. Expressions of fear, tiredness, or tension can be present. At this stage, supplying your horse with rest, food, and water usually counters the fatigue.

Note: In the beginning stages of exhaustion, symptoms are overlooked in our excitement while riding. Pay attention to your horse often and learn to take vital signs during times of increased exertion or when you sense something is abnormal.

As his exhaustion increases in severity, electrolyte imbalances happen because of heavy sweating. Tying up, a condition where the muscles become painful or stiff due to multiple factors, may occur. Under heavy exertion, the heart and respiration rates will be well above normal and often will not return to normal rates at rest. During extreme effort, the respiration rate may become faster than the heart rate. This creates a breathing pattern called "thumps" (synchronous diaphragmatic flutter), where the diaphragm contracts in time with the heartbeat, shaking the entire animal and giving him a rapid, inefficient breathing pattern.

If this occurs, stop the animal immediately and begin a cooling-down process. Offer water and electrolytes after the animal has settled down. The horse will be done for the day and will need a long rest period, giving special attention to his water, electrolytes, and feed. Monitor him closely.

Well into the severe stage, the horse will not cool down, and his temperature may rise above 106°F with no sweating. When a thermometer is inserted to take the rectal temperature, the anus muscles may be loose, possibly allowing air to enter the rectum. Urine output can be decreased due to kidney shutdown, and feces may be drier. Death could possibly occur without medical intervention at this late stage.

Remember, mild exhaustion is common while riding in steep, rugged terrain, so stop your horse often and allow him to cool off and rest as necessary. Monitor his demeanor, heart rate, and breathing rate, and observe whether he is sweating. Also, let your horse drink as often as he wants.

Severe exhaustion isn't common in horses while trail riding, and there's usually another underlying problem if this occurs. As I already mentioned, conditioning your horse beforehand to ward off injury works the best. The adage, "An ounce of prevention is worth a pound of cure," is good advice.

Horse Vital Signs and Condition

Learning to monitor your horse's vital signs accurately is essential because they indicate the horse's health and physical condition, whether normal or abnormal. Note: This chart is for adult horses, and all vitals must be taken fifteen minutes after rest from working and out of the sun. The horse should be calm with nothing causing agitation to the animal. It's equally important that every horse owner know his or her horses normal, healthy resting temperature, heart rate, and respiration rate for comparison. Mildly abnormal vital signs while at rest should be monitored closely. Moderate to severe vital signs at rest warrants an immediate call or visit to the veterinarian.

Vital Sign	Normal	Moderate	Severe
Heart Rate (bpm)	28-44	44-69	70-80
Respiratory Rate (bpm)	12 to 24	24 to 40	above 40
Temperature	98° to 101.5°	101.5° to 103°	above 104°

Capillary refill time: Press your finger firmly against the horse's gums and remove quickly. The point of pressure should return to a pink color within one to two seconds. Longer refill times indicate poor blood profusion.

Intestinal sounds: Gurgling, clicks, growls, squeaks, and occasional roars are normal. Decreased or absent intestinal sounds can be a sign of colic, especially if the horse is biting at its side, rolling, lying down, or otherwise seems to be in distress.

Attitude: Healthy horses are bright and alert and are interested in other horses and their surroundings.

Eyes: Horse's eyes should be bright, fully open, and clean, not cloudy or discolored. Any indications of unusual discharge or a dull, glazed appearance should warrant a DVM checkup.

Nose: The nostrils should be clean and free of excessive mucus. However, it is normal for a horse to have a trickle of clear liquid from the nostrils.

Mucous membranes: The horse's gums should be moist and a healthy shade of pink.

Appetite: Decreased appetite is typical in an overheated horse. But once the horse has rested, reluctance to eat is an indication of infectious diseases such as influenza or the West Nile virus. In some cases, tooth problems may prevent eating, so to differentiate, take the horse's rectal temperature. An adult horse at rest should have a body temperature of 99-101.5°F. Anything above that level can indicate an active infection. Be sure to obtain his temperature while the horse has a long rest period out of the sun.

Hair coat: A shiny, glowing coat is a sign of good health that comes from meeting the horse's nutritional requirements. A dull coat can be a sign of poor nutrition, parasites, or generally poor health.

Weight: Over/underweight horses can have health issues or be at an increased risk of injury. Use the Henneke Body Condition nine-level scoring system to evaluate your horse's body condition. A body condition score of four to five is ideal.

Manure: A healthy horse will pass manure eight to twelve times a day.

Urine: Should be wheat-colored and either clear or slightly cloudy.

Hydration: The average horse drinks between five and ten gallons of water per day. Exercise and weather conditions can significantly affect intake.

Legs and feet: The horse should stand on all four feet easily without abnormal positioning—parked out, standing under, or lameness. It's normal for a hind leg to be at rest. The horse should gait freely and confidently.

NATIONAL GEOGRAPHIC

Tennessee
North Carolina

229

Great Smoky Mountains
National Park

TRAILS ILLUSTRATED
TOPOGRAPHIC MAP

REVISED REGULARLY
WATERPROOF • TEAR RESISTANT

NAVIGATION

This guidebook provides a general layout of the trail you will be riding with important written descriptions to help you locate paths. You could use it alone, but having one of the maps noted below in conjunction with this guide will provide very confident navigation.

Maps

A National Geographic Trails illustrated map is an accurate tool to carry along because it is revised regularly in cooperation with the National Park Service. All hiking and horse trails are accurately represented on waterproof paper which is tear-resistant. They can be purchased at the park's visitor centers and ranger stations. If you would like to order one before your arrival for study, you may contact the publisher by phone at (800)-962-1643 or visit online at www.nationalgeographic.com.

A smaller map, referred to as the Great Smoky Mountains Trail Map, provides rules and regulations for horses. It also includes information helpful to horsemen. Brochures for horseback riding and camping can be found in the park's visitor centers.

Compass

Another useful tool to bring along is a high-quality compass. It is the best and most dependable tool to stay accurately oriented in unfamiliar and changing terrain. Learn to use it without questioning the accuracy.

Lensatic compass.

Global Positioning System (GPS)

The Global Positioning System is a handy tool, especially with today's technology. One was utilized in the creation of this book, which is accurate to one foot but don't rely on it alone. All GPS products use the same or similar satellite support bases. The quality of the reception keeps it on track via the satellites' signals. Higher-priced units usually are the best at maintaining good reception; however, antennas can be purchased for different models to extend the range. Keep in mind, the park has many high mountain peaks and low valleys, causing hindered reception. Thick tree canopies, tight ravines, and towering trees also block reception of radio signals. It is always best to navigate with simple maps and tools not requiring batteries or technology.

Global Positioning System.

USING THIS GUIDE

his book follows a basic, easy-to-understand format. Refer to it often to avoid problematic encounters and to gain a better perspective before traveling to the park with your trailer loaded. Also, horse-related topics have been added to increase your knowledge and pleasure. Purchase a map of the GSMNP, place it inside this guide, and carry them both in your saddlebag. This combination will provide optimal navigation. Some of the information throughout the text is redundant to help you reduce having to search.

Routes are made up of multiple **trails**.

A **Rider Skill Level** has been assigned to the overall **route.**

The **routes** are graded as *Easy, Moderate, Difficult*, or *Extreme* for the rider. Most of the routes in the Cades Cove area are rugged and fall between a *Moderate* to *Difficult* rating. There were no *Extreme* level trails, only small segments which may be extreme to some have been encountered at Cades Cove.

Also, just because the overall **route** is graded as *Moderate* or *Difficult* does not mean some of the individual **trails** of the route are considered difficult. There are some easy trails and many effortless segments to relax on while riding. If you become fearful on a seemingly dangerous segment, you can always lead your horse through those areas or return after you gain more confidence.

Each trail was ridden and evaluated to help inform horsemen of dangers, problems, or hindrances not listed in any other literature. **Be**

aware, though, every detail could not be added as the info would be overwhelming and possibly spoil the ride.

A horse rating system was also utilized which grades the amount of effort needed by a healthy, average-size horse. The levels are ***Easy, Moderate, Strenuous***, and ***Very Strenuous***. Keep in mind that a horse's abilities vary due to factors such as age, size, health, weight carried, and whether the horse is exercised regularly. It is your responsibility to know your horse's physical abilities or limitations before venturing into a wilderness on long, rugged trails.

Planning Your Trip

It's easy to forget things while planning a great trip out with your horses. Many preparations for your horse and yourself must be well-thought-out in advance. So, before you visit, make sure to utilize books like this one, videos, and websites. The Great Smoky Mountain National Park website is an excellent place to start. Once you arrive in the park, stop by one of the visitor centers to get a copy of the seasonal Smoky Mountains Guides, which will provide information about the park, ranger-led programs, and other recommendations for things to do. Also, there are many interesting books found at the visitor center. Learning about the plants, animals, and history will significantly enrich your visit while you ride along.

Know where the Parking Areas are Located

Spence Field/Russell Field, Crib Gap, and Rich Mountain Loop trails can be accessed from the day parking area or from the Anthony Creek Horse Camp, as they are located near the entrance of Cades Cove. Middle Prong Trail cannot since it's located several miles away near Tremont.

Abrams Falls Loop and Gregory Bald Trail are located on the opposite side of the Cove. You must travel inside the ever-popular and busy loop of Cades Cove to reach those trailheads. Much patience

Parking area for Middle Prong Trail near Tremont.

will be required because of the many tourists who come to see the wildlife. If a wild animal is sighted, you and your horse may have to endure an hour or more on a one-way road. There will be nowhere to turn around either. Sparks Lane and Hyatt Lane will provide the only shortcuts out on the eleven-mile loop if you decide to cancel your ride. Average time around the entire loop road during busy periods is two to four hours.

When exiting after riding, you will again encounter many tourists. Waiting in traffic for one or two hours, with a hot and tired horse loaded in your trailer, must be expected. Careful diligence on your part can help you plan a suitable time when the road is less congested so you can venture onto those trails. Usually, early mornings and late afternoons are best. Don't plan rides on holidays in order to avoid tourists.

Cades Cove day parking area near the entrance for Spence Field/Russell Field, Crib Gap, and Rich Mountain Loop trails.

Access to Anthony Creek Trailhead which leads to Spence Field/Russell Field Loop passing through the center of the Anthony Creek Horse Camp.

Abrams Creek has a relatively large parking area.

Small parking area for Gregory Bald Trail on Parsons Branch Road. Always check with the backcountry rangers before planning to ride at this location. The road is almost always closed.

Trails Accessible from Anthony Creek Horse Camp

Trailheads you can reach from Anthony Creek Horse Camp in this guide are Crib Gap Loop, Spence Field/Russell Field Loop, and Rich Mountain Loop.

Additional trails can be located on the map of these same routes to make your own paths.

Note: the trail routes listed in this guide are the most commonly traveled.

THE TRAILS

Before climbing in the saddle, be ready for the ride.

Miry Ridge Trail just as the morning sun breaks.

The distance traveled from six routes listed in this guide, including the short leg to the trailheads, equals near seventy miles on twenty-three trails.

1. Middle Prong 2.3
2. Panther Creek 2.3
3. Miry Ridge 2.5
4. Lynn Camp Prong 3.7
5. Middle Prong (remaining section) 1.8
6. Anthony Creek 3.5
7. Bote Mountain 1.7
8. Appalachian Trail 2.9
9. Russell Field 3.5
10. Anthony Creek (remaining section) 1.6
11. Crib Gap 1.6
12. Turkey Pen Ridge 3.4
13. Schoolhouse Gap 2.3
14. Finley Cane 2.8
15. Rich Mountain 2.9
16. Indian Grave 2.0
17. Crooked Arm Ridge 2.2
18. Wet Bottom 1.0
19. Cooper Road 5.5
20. Hatcher Mountain 4.5
21. Rabbit Creek 5.1
22. Gregory Bald 4.1

MIDDLE PRONG LOOP

Encompassing Trails: Middle Prong, Panther Creek, Miry Ridge,
Lynn Camp Prong

Trail Features: This track features some of the best waterfalls early on and produces the most prolific mountain laurel slicks found within this guide. Also, there are numerous smaller falls and cascades to behold. Sights off the Miry Ridge Trail at the rocky point are inspiring. Laurel blooms starting in late May through June are showy, and you will ride through many enchanting laurel tunnels.

Parking and Trailhead Location: The Middle Prong Trailhead is located near Townsend at Tremont. Coming from Townsend, turn right at the "Y" intersection onto Laurel Creek Road. Then, turn left off Laurel Creek onto Tremont Road. You will pass the Great Smoky Mountains Institute at Tremont after two miles. Continue another three miles past the institute on a gravel road that dead-ends at the trailhead. The parking area is roughly laid out like a cul-de-sac.

Need to Know Information: This track is the only one not located immediately at or inside Cades Cove.

Start early to avoid traffic on Laurel Creek and the gravel portion of the road leading to the Tremont parking area. A two-horse trailer is required for maneuvering on the small, winding road. Also, be prepared to cross multiple, one-lane bridges. At one of the bridges, the road has a sharp left bend immediately before the bridge, making it impossible to pass with an extended trailer. Do not attempt.

The parking area is not well designed, so you must get there early to locate a parking space large enough to accommodate your rig. Many tourists visit this trail because of the easy access to the waterfalls. They will quickly fill the parking lot in the morning and block the few spaces large enough for trucks and trailers.

Begin: Travel from the parking area and cross the long metal bridge where you will immediately find the trailhead sign.

Distance: Fifteen miles

Average Time: Six to seven hours. Longer for groups or slow animals.

Elevation Gained: 2,985 ft. (Max. elevation 4,665 ft.)

Trail Type: Mixed mountain soil with many rocks and roots. There are multiple stream crossings, but they are not wide. The trail starts wide but changes to narrow single track throughout much of the route.

Rider Skill Level: *Moderate* to *Difficult*. There are many rocks and roots, which can cause the horse to stumble. Narrow ledges will be encountered on segments of the trail. Attempting to cross Panther Creek after heavy rains can be impassable or hazardous. Coaching a lesser-skilled rider on this route can be accomplished with a well-mannered, experienced horse.

Horse Effort: *Strenuous*. Sturdy, healthy horses and mules are desirable because of the long inclines, uneven terrain, and the overall gain in altitude. Pacing your animal will be required.

Trail Precautions: Horses recommended to be shod or wear boots for foot protection. This trail has the potential for pulling a shoe or a boot. Hikers will be encountered at various points, especially at the beginning and ending of Middle Prong Trail. The long, narrow, high bridge must be crossed at the beginning to reach the trailhead. Panther Creek and

Miry Ridge trails have some narrow paths near ledges. Avoid Panther Creek crossing during times of flooding.

Resources: Water is abundant, and grass can be found along the trail. Camping is available at Campsite 28 on Lynn Camp Prong.. A backcountry permit must be obtained by calling the Backcountry Office prior to camping (865-436-1297).

Nearest Town: Townsend, TN

Fees and Permits: No fees. Must have Coggins test available upon park ranger's request.

Seasons: Currently open year-round except Christmas. Riding is discouraged, but not closed, during the winter months because of increased chances of trail erosion or damage.

The Ride

This route will travel clockwise, ascending the harder section first, while the Lynn Camp Prong Trail will be easier as you descend.

Proceed from the parking area and cross the long bridge. You will see the trailhead sign straight ahead. There is a path on the right of the sign, which is misleading. Do not take it. Stay left, traveling alongside the creek on the extra-wide trail for 2.3 miles. There will be many scenic views of the creek with numerous waterfalls and cascades. Other sights will include large boulders and laurel slicks.

Caution: Many tourists will be encountered on this section of the ride during busy hours, and you will return down this same path after making the loop, encountering them again.

Once you reach the first trail intersection, turn left, immediately crossing Panther Creek to a narrow, rocky path. There are tripping hazards from the numerous rocks and roots on the Panther Creek Trail. Continue for another 2.3 miles through massive laurel slicks and small streams. The grade will increase slightly.

Jakes Gap's four-way intersection will be noticeable by the flat area once you reach it. Turn right, traveling uphill on Miry Ridge Trail for 2.5 miles. Along this section, the grade will increase, where you will cross higher ledges until you reach the top. You will experience the best mountain sights from this portion of the ride. Nearing the end of Miry Ridge Trail, Campsite 26 for hikers will be on the left.

Turn right at the intersection of Lynn Camp Prong Trail and Miry Ridge. You will notice the trail losing grade and becoming better, with fewer rocks and roots. Travel about two miles until you reach what appears to be another trail intersection, but isn't. This is near Campsite 28 for horses. The path to the right will lead to the horse camp. The path to the left will keep you on Lynn Camp Prong Trail.

Caution: Some people have been misled here because this section is not accurately portrayed on the maps.

Once you come to the end of Lynn Camp Prong Trail, turn right at this intersection, which will be the upper portion of the Middle Prong Trail (the trail you started on). It is noticeable by the wider path. Left is the Green Briar Trail, leading up the mountain to the Appalachian Trail. After making a right onto the Middle Prong, travel 1.8 miles, encountering several switchbacks. There will be numerous shortcuts, but stay on course until you reach the trail intersection at Panther Creek. The loop will now be complete. Travel down the extra-wide Middle Prong Trail again back to the parking area.

Middle Prong Trailhead sign.

Panther Creek.

Miry Ridge Trail.

SPENCE FIELD / RUSSELL FIELD LOOP

Encompassing trails: Anthony Creek, Bote Mountain, Appalachian Trail, and Russell Field

Trail Features: During the late spring and early summer, blooms of mountain laurel and rhododendron will be sprinkled throughout this route, and many charming streams can be admired along the way. Beautiful grass meadows at Spence Field provide an excellent place for a picnic. Panoramic views through the trees of the North Carolina mountains and valley are visible from the higher elevations.

Parking and Trailhead Location: From Townsend, TN, turn right onto Laurel Creek Road at the "Y" intersection to Cades Cove. You will travel west over seven miles and arrive at the Cove. Turn left toward the camping area just before entering the Cades Cove Loop Road. Travel a short distance, and turn right on the first paved road. The parking area will be in view on the left. The trailhead is located at the back of Anthony Creek Horse Camp.

Need to Know Information: Start early to avoid traffic on Laurel Creek Road to Cades Cove. Heavy traffic will be unavoidable if you trailer out in the middle of the day after the ride. Departing late is ideal. If hauling at peak hours, expect to wait in stop-and-go traffic and possibly encounter no parking availability. A two-horse trailer is better for maneuvering on the small, winding road to the Cove. Also, the maximum trailer size is about twenty-four feet for the parking area, and the spacing is limited to three or four rigs. Beware—the parking area is not assigned to any group, nor does it have signs indicating it's a parking area. Additionally, parking is on a first-come-first-serve basis, and all visitors can use it. If you mistakenly enter the Cove Loop Road, you will not be able to turn around or back out because it's one-way, and there will be traffic behind you.

There are no signs from the parking area pointing the way to the trailhead. To reach the trailhead, walk your horse across the road you came in on, and find the narrow path along the right side. Travel a short distance and make a right into the Cades Cove picnic area. Continue traveling straight on the one-way road through the picnic area. At the back, you will come to a gate, which most likely will be closed but not locked. Go around the gate, continuing down the gravel path until you pass Crib Gap Trailhead on the left. The horse camp will be within view, and the trailhead will be on the far side of camp.

You will encounter many park visitors before reaching the Anthony Creek trail head, so use caution walking through the picnic area. Park officials require you to lead your horse through this area for safety reasons. Likewise, use caution while crossing the road from the parking lot because there can be heavy traffic.

If you would like to avoid the day parking area, you can reserve a space at the Anthony Creek Horse Camp which is right at the trailhead. There are three available trailer spaces. To reserve, go online to https://www.recreation.gov or call 877-444-6777.

Begin: Travel from the day parking area unless camped at Anthony Creek Horse Camp.

Distance: 13.3 miles

Average Time: Five to six hours. Longer for groups or slow animals.

Elevation Gained: 2,927 ft. (Max. elevation 5023 ft.)

Rider Skill Level: *Moderate* to *Difficult*. There are many rocks and roots which can cause stumbling. Riding along narrow ledges will occur while both descending and ascending. Short wooden bridges and streams must be crossed. Coaching a lesser-skilled rider on this route can be achieved with a well-mannered, experienced horse.

Horse Effort: *Strenuous*. Sturdy, healthy horses are desirable because of the long incline and the overall gain in altitude. Pacing your horse will be required.

Trail Type: Mixed mountain soil with many rocks and roots. There are several stream crossings, but they are not wide. Trail width is mostly wide track but has some single track.

Trail Precautions: Horses recommended to be shod or have boots for protection. Hikers will be encountered at various points. There are some small bridges. Use caution on stream crossings during heavy rains.

Resources: Water is abundant along the ride, and so is grass at Spence Field for your horse. Camping is available at both Spence and Russell Field shelters, equipped with hitching posts. Camping at those sites will be shared with the hikers on the AT. A backcountry permit must be obtained by calling the Backcountry Office before camping (865-436-1297).

Nearest Town: Townsend, TN

Fees and Permits: No fees. Must have Coggins test available upon ranger's request.

Seasons: Currently open year-round except Christmas. Riding is discouraged, but not closed, during the winter months because of increased chances of trail erosion or damage.

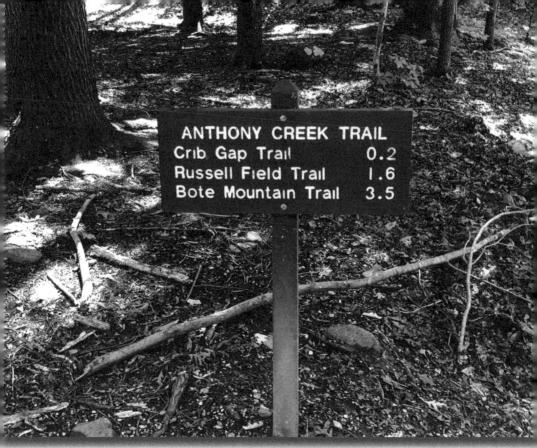

ANTHONY CREEK TRAIL
Crib Gap Trail   0.2
Russell Field Trail   1.6
Bote Mountain Trail   3.5

Anthony Creek Trailhead sign.

The Ride

The route will travel clockwise, climbing the steeper grade first. Once you reach the top of the mountain, the remainder of the route will mostly descend.

Proceed at the trailhead and climb steadily along All-Night Ridge, following the creek for about three to four miles. Small bridges and creek crossings will be encountered early on. At 1.6 miles, you will come to a split in the trail, with Russell Field Trail being on the right. Anthony Creek Trail will continue left; therefore, go left at this intersection. Bote Mountain intersection will be reached in 1.9 miles. Along this section, you will see a footpath leading to a campsite for hikers on the right, but it is not the trail. Continue straight. The camp can be seen by looking down the footpath, which lies near the creek on a clear, flat area.

After reaching the Bote Mountain intersection, turn right onto Bote Mountain Trail and travel another 1.7 miles. On clear days, there will be partial views of Cades Cove through the trees. Also, portions of this trail are deeply carved into the crest from cattle being driven up the bald more than a century ago. Thus, the name was given to the grassy bald from the person who did this—Gregory Spence.

As you near the Appalachian Trail junction near the top, the trail will begin to level out some, and you will start to notice grassy patches mixed among the trees. Turn right onto the AT, and travel a short distance until you see a sign pointing to the Spence Field backcountry shelter on the left. If you want to take a break, this area makes for an excellent place to rest and enjoy the views at Spence Field. You don't have to travel far, and it's well worth seeing. The shelter is open to camping with your horse.

After a break, return to the AT and make a left, getting back on the route. The AT section of trail will be single track and provide partial views of the North Carolina side of the Smoky Mountains. During this stretch of the AT trail, you will pass Maple Sugar Gap and McCampbell Knob. You will pass through long tunnels of mountain laurel, making for a pleasant experience. Russell Field will be reached in another 2.9 miles. Once you

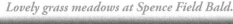

Lovely grass meadows at Spence Field Bald.

reach the Russell Field intersection, you will be at the shelter. There are hitching posts if you want to take another break before descending the mountain, and you can also camp here with horses.

Take a right in front of the shelter onto Russell Field Trail, and continue downhill for another 3.5 miles. Along this path, you will see another campsite for hikers, but stay straight on Russell Field Trail. Once you reach the Anthony Creek Trail intersection, you will have completed the loop. Continue for the remainder of the path to complete the ride.

Entering one of the many water crossings.

CRIB GAP TRAIL

← Turkeypen Ridge Trail

ANTHONY CREEK TRAIL   0.2

◄ Trailhead

► Russell Field Trail   1.

► Bote Mountain   3.

CRIB GAP LOOP

Encompassing Trails: Crib Gap, Turkey Pen Ridge, Schoolhouse Gap, Bote Mountain, Finley Cane

Trail Features: This route doesn't take you deep into the wilderness, but it has some excellent features. In the beginning, mountain laurel will be strewn along the wooded path while you travel parallel to Laurel Creek Road. A narrow ridgeline forest can be enjoyed, with sedge grasses growing in the bottoms. Bote Mountain Trail has some beautiful views off the ridgeline, and tulip poplar trees make Finley Cane a delight.

Parking and Trailhead Location: From Townsend, TN, turn right onto Laurel Creek Road at the "Y" intersection to Cades Cove. You will travel west over seven miles and arrive at the Cove. Turn left toward the camping area just before entering the Cades Cove Loop Road. Travel a short distance, and turn right on the first paved road. The parking area will be in view on the left. The trailhead is located at the back of Anthony Creek Horse Camp.

Need to Know Information: Turkey Pen Ridge Trail is a single, narrow track winding along the side of a ridge. There are numerous ledges and narrow soft shoulders along its entire length, which can be dangerous for a rider with a flighty or unsteady horse. Turkey Pen Ridge Trail can be avoided while enjoying the easier encompassing trails if one desires.

This route takes you along Laurel Creek Road, where you will cross the busy road multiple times. Extreme caution must be used while crossing with your horse because there are no signs or pedestrian crosswalks to assist with crossing safely.

The road crossing at Schoolhouse Gap Trail is the most hazardous to pedestrians. You must lead your horse along a path beside the road near oncoming traffic while crossing a high bridge. After the bridge, you must then cross the road to continue the trail, while oncoming traffic is coming out of a blind curve. There is very little space to allow for reaction time, making it difficult for motorists to avoid you. I've evaluated this path multiple times and have found it to be very dangerous because you and your horse are within two feet of oncoming traffic. The locals have informed me of a horse that was killed at this location and another which was severely injured. Even calm horses will be apprehensive crossing the bridge because of the proximity of the passing vehicles.

Horseback riders have diverted from the intended path, going up the bank beside it instead of crossing it. To find this bypass, look for the path leading across the stream a short piece before reaching the parking area at the road. You will ford the stream and climb on the far side of the bridge, thereby removing the need to cross it alongside the road. Once you're at the roadside, motorists will approach you from a blind curve on the left. They usually are traveling fast in their excitement to reach Cades Cove. Use extreme caution, and don't try to be in a hurry. If you must, employ someone to stop traffic for you.

Start early to avoid traffic on Laurel Creek Road while trailering to Cades Cove. Heavy traffic will be unavoidable if you trailer out in the middle of the day—departing late is best. If hauling at peak hours, expect to wait in stop-and-go traffic and possibly encounter no parking availability. A two-horse trailer is better for maneuvering on the narrow, winding road to the Cove. Also, the maximum trailer size is about twenty-four feet for the parking area, and the spacing is limited to three or four rigs. The parking area is not designated to any group, nor does it have signs indicating it's a parking area. Additionally, parking is on a first-come-first-serve basis, and other visitors can use it. If you mistakenly enter the Cove Loop Road, you will not be able to turn around or back out because it's one-way, and there will be traffic behind you.

There are no signs from the parking area pointing the way to the trailhead. You will need to go back on the road you came in on and look for a narrow path on the right side of the road. Travel a short distance, and make a right into the Cades Cove picnic area. Continue traveling straight on the one-way road through the picnic area. At the back, you will come to a gate, which most likely will be closed but not locked. Go around the gate, continuing down the gravel path until you come to Crib Gap Trailhead on the left. Anthony Creek Horse Camp can be seen from the trailhead.

Many visitors will be encountered before reaching the trailhead, so use caution walking through the picnic area. Park officials require you to lead your horse through this area for safety reasons. Likewise, use caution while crossing the road from the parking lot because there can be heavy traffic.

If you would like to avoid the day parking area, you can reserve a spot at the Anthony Creek Horse Camp which is near the trailhead. There are three available trailer spaces. To book, go online to https://www.recreation.gov or call 877-444-6777.

Begin: Travel from the day parking area unless camped at Anthony Creek Horse Camp.

Distance: Twelve miles

Average Time: Five to six hours

Elevation Gained: 667 ft. (Max. elevation 2209)

Rider Skill Level: *Moderate* to *Difficult*. Turkey Pen Ridge Trail can be difficult for inexperienced riders because of the narrow ledges. Also, rocks and roots can cause stumbling near these ledges that have soft shoulders. The other encompassing trails are easy to moderate and can be enjoyed if you want to avoid Turkey Pen Ridge. Another difficulty is managing your horse crossing the busy Laurel Creek Road.

Horse Effort: *Moderate*. Pacing your horse may be needed. This route is the least strenuous of all the routes.

Trail Type: Mixed mountain soil with rocks and roots. There are several stream crossings, but they are not wide. Trail width is mostly wide track, but Turkey Pen Ridge is a narrow, single track.

Trail Precautions: Horses recommended to be shod or have boots for protection. Hikers will be encountered at various points. Use caution on Turkey Pen Ridge and crossing the roads. Ledges will be encountered.

Resources: Water is abundant along the ride

Nearest Town: Townsend, TN

Fees and Permits: No fees. Must have Coggins test available upon ranger's request.

Seasons: Currently open year-round except Christmas. Riding is discouraged, but not closed, during the winter months because of increased chances of trail erosion or damage.

Turkey Pen Ridge Trail.

Dangerous road crossing on Schoolhouse Gap Trail.

The Ride

This route will travel clockwise and tour the harder section first, with a pleasant stroll through the cove hardwoods near the end.

Proceed from the day parking area until you reach the trailhead sign, and turn left onto Crib Gap Trail. Travel about thirty minutes through the wooded area until you reach Laurel Creek Road. Cross the road and walk about thirty yards along the shoulder until you see the trail continuing downhill.

After a short trek, you will arrive at a four-way intersection. Turn left, traveling to Schoolhouse Gap on Turkey Pen Ridge Trail. You will cross a stream and begin climbing on a narrow path near a ledge. Soft shoulder ledges will be encountered at various portions throughout its length. Mixed timber forest with mountain laurel and rhododendron make up much of the trail while traversing in and out of the dry flanks and moist hollows.

After a 3.4-mile ride on Turkey Pen, you will come to a three-way intersection, which will be Schoolhouse Gap Trail. Turn right, and travel down the wide path about twenty minutes. You will soon come to the stream near Laurel Creek Road. The road, bridge, and a small parking area will also come into view.

Caution: This crossing is dangerous during heavy traffic. Injuries and fatalities have occurred at this location. The correct trail path leads you to the parking area and to the road. Once at the road, turn left and walk a narrow path beside the road and cross the bridge. After the bridge, you will then cross the road to continue on the trail.

Taking the safer path is a far better option than risking injury. Instead of going to the road and crossing the bridge, find the bypass just before the parking area, and cross the creek. Look for horse tracks leading into the creek and on the opposite side going up the bank beside the bridge. There is a well-worn path beside the bridge which brings you onto the shoulder of Laurel Creek Road. The trail will then be just across the road, with a sign indicating West Prong Trail is 1.2 miles away. You must use caution crossing the road because there is a blind curve on the left, and there is no pedestrian crosswalk. Tourists are usually in a hurry to Cades Cove and will not slow down. If you must, employ someone to block traffic while you cross the road with your horse. Once you cross the road, continue until reaching Bote Mountain Trail.

Turn right onto Bote Mountain Trail, and travel uphill for a short trek until you reach the Finley Cane Trail intersection on the right. There are some nice views through the tree line off Bote Mountain Trail.

Turn right onto Finley Cane, and travel 2.8 miles through a nice cove hardwood forest with many tall tulip poplar trees. There will be a hitching post within a mile if you choose to take a break. Near the end of Finley Cane, you will ride through many laurel slicks and cross a few streams. Soon, you will be close to Laurel Creek Road again. When you reach the forest sign indicating Turkey Pen Ridge Trail and Crib Gap 0.2 miles away, stay left and soon cross a small stream beside the road. Go a short way beside the road and cross Laurel Creek Road again to the right. After traveling 0.2 miles and reaching the Crib Gap forest sign, the loop will be complete. Turn left onto Crib Gap, and travel back to the trailhead where you first started.

Crib Gap Trail.

Tulip poplar trees on Finley Cane.

RICH MOUNTAIN LOOP

Encompassing Trails: Rich Mountain, Indian Grave Gap, and Crooked Arm Ridge

Trail Features: Grassy meadows can be enjoyed on the first section of this ride where deer, turkey, and bear can often be spotted roaming. Before ascending the mountain from the field, you will see the John Oliver Cabin, which is one of the oldest structures within the park. One interesting fact about Mr. Oliver is that he delivered mail via horseback in the nineteenth century to the residents of the Cove. As you begin to climb, nice views of Cades Cove will come into view through the tree line. After you summit, there will be high views overlooking the Townsend and Tuckaleechee area. Mountain laurel and flame azaleas are sprinkled along the way, and so are wild flowers. Nice mountain views, ravines, and a waterfall are part of the scenery on this route.

Parking and Trailhead Location: From Townsend, TN, turn right onto Laurel Creek Road at the "Y" intersection to Cades Cove. You will travel west over seven miles and arrive at the Cove. Turn left toward the camping area just before entering the Cades Cove Loop Road. Travel a short distance, and turn right on the first paved road. The parking area will be in view on the left. The trailhead will be found on the right side of the Cades Cove Loop Road just as you enter.

Need to Know Information: Start early to avoid traffic on Laurel Creek Road to Cades Cove. Heavy traffic will be unavoidable if you trailer out in the middle of the day unless departing late. If hauling at peak hours, expect to wait in stop-and-go traffic and possibly encounter no parking availability. A two-horse trailer is better for maneuvering on the small, winding road to the Cove. Also, the maximum trailer size is about twenty-four feet for the parking area, and the spacing is limited to three or four rigs. Beware—the parking area is not assigned to any group, nor does it have signs indicating it's a parking area. Additionally, parking is on a first-come-first-serve basis, and other visitors can use it. If you mistakenly enter the Cove Loop Road, you will not be able to turn around or back out because it's one-way, and there will be traffic behind you.

There are no signs from the parking area pointing the way to the trailhead; therefore, travel through the orange-and-white gate beside where you are parked. Gate may be closed. If so, go around and travel a short distance until you reach a footpath on the right going uphill to the Cade's Cove Information Kiosk's parking area. Proceed up the hill to the busy Cades Cove Loop Road entrance. The trailhead will be just on the other side of the road in viewing range as you enter the loop. Use caution crossing the road during heavy traffic times.

Begin: Travel from the day parking area to the trailhead beside Cades Cove Loop Road unless camped at Anthony Creek Horse Camp

Distance: 8.9 miles

Average Time: Three to four-and-a-half hours. Longer for groups or slow animals.

Elevation Gained: 1827 ft. (Max. elevation 3638 ft.)

Trail Type: Mostly wide track but has some narrow sections. Mixed mountain soil types with a few outcroppings of rocks. Has small, shallow stream crossings.

Rider Skill Level: *Moderate* to *Difficult*. Rider must safely guide horse near a few brief high ledges on Rich Mountain trail; however, a lesser-skilled rider can lead their horse at these sections with a well-mannered, experienced horse.

RICH MOUNTAIN LOOP TRAIL
Crooked Arm Ridge Trail 0.5
Indian Grave Gap Trail   3.4

Rich Mountain
Trailhead sign.

Horse Effort: *Strenuous*. Sturdy, healthy horses and mules are desirable because of the long inclines and the overall gain in altitude. Pacing your horse will be required.

Trail Precautions: Horses recommended to be shod or have boots for protection. Hikers will be encountered at various points. Use caution crossing Cades Cove Loop Road and riding near the ledges.

Fees and Permits: No fees. Must have Coggins test available upon ranger's request.

Seasons: Currently open year-round except Christmas. Riding is discouraged, but not closed, during the winter months because of increased chances of trail erosion or damage.

The Ride

This route will travel clockwise and tour the steeper section first up Rich Mountain and descend with nice views off Crooked Arm Trail.

Proceed to Cades Cove Loop Road from the parking area. Cross the road and enter at the trailhead immediately on the right. The first trail intersection will be about half a mile away and will be where you complete the loop from Crooked Arm Ridge Trail. Stay left on the Rich Mountain Loop Trail as it skirts along the wood-line around the back of open fields. You will reach the John Oliver Cabin in about 1.4 miles. At the cabin, veer hard right and begin climbing the mountain steadily. Indian Grave Gap junction will be roughly two miles away.

As you steadily climb, the trail will become increasingly narrow and steeper with a few high ledges. You will encounter multiple switchbacks while gaining altitude. Use caution—this section contains the steepest

grades. Continue until you reach the Indian Grave Gap intersection, and turn right. You will begin to notice a lessening of the grade and widening of the trail beyond this point.

Travel .8 miles on Indian Grave Gap Trail until you reach another intersection. Turn right, and ride along the crest of Rich Mountain. The trail will be wide and mostly straight with some nice high views of the Townsend and Tuckaleechee Cove area. Cades Cove will come into view at various points on the right.

Proceed traveling northward on Indian Grave Trail until you come to another intersection. Scott Mountain Trail branches left which is for hiking only, while Crooked Arm Ridge Trail branches right. Go right, which will continue down the mountain. There will be a few narrow portions with switchbacks on this section but not as steep as the ride up. Nice wooded ravines are pleasant along this portion, and a cascading waterfall can be enjoyed.

After passing the waterfall, you will soon come to the last trail junction. It will be the first one you passed near the beginning of the ride and will complete the loop. Turn left at this junction, which will lead back to the Cove entrance and the parking area.

John Oliver's cabin.

ABRAMS CREEK LOOP

Encompassing Trails: Wet Bottom, Cooper Road, Hatcher Mountain, Rabbit Creek

Trail Features: You can stroll through pine-oak laden forests on rolling ridges while enjoying many rhododendron and mountain laurel shrubs. Sights from Hatcher Mountain Trail produce some splended views of the surrounding hills. Abrams Creek is a refreshing delight near the halfway point.

The track will also take you along what was originally an old Native American path which the first settlers used to enter the Cove. Now known as Cooper Road, it allowed access to Maryville, where supplies were purchased and brought back via horse and wagon in the 1830s.

Parking and Trailhead Location: From Townsend, TN, turn right onto Laurel Creek Road at the "Y" intersection to Cades Cove. You will travel west over seven miles and arrive at the entrance to the Cove Loop Road. Enter the loop and travel to the far side until you see the gravel road on the right leading to Abrams Falls Trailhead. The large open gravel parking area has a vault toilet in the center.

Need to Know Information: You'll find this trail located within Cades Cove near the halfway point on the eleven-mile loop road.

Cades Cove Loop Road is closed for bicycle and foot traffic every Saturday and Wednesday morning until 10 a.m. from early May until late

September. Otherwise, the road is open year-round to motor vehicles from sunrise until sunset daily, weather permitting.

Start early to avoid heavy traffic on Laurel Creek and Cades Cove Loop Roads. A two-horse trailer is better for maneuvering on the small, narrow, winding road. Do not attempt towing a large trailer. The gate opens thirty minutes after first light, and there will be a line already forming before it opens. You will need copious amounts of patience before reaching Abrams Trailhead, especially if you start later in the day. The road is a one-way/one-lane paved road. It may take over an hour to travel seven miles in slow, stop-and-go traffic. If you decide to exit before reaching the trailhead, you will need to take one of the shortcut roads, either Sparks Lane or Hyatt Lane. The best way to avoid the delays on the loop road will be by getting in line before daylight and exiting late in the evening. Gates close at dark.

Caution: Because of the remote area and limited access, this trail can cause a very delayed emergency response to both you or your horse. Expect that no one will get to you soon in such an event. Likewise, if you encounter a problem while trailering into the Cove, expect a long wait for help to arrive.

Old Barn.

Begin: Travel from the parking area to the Abrams Falls Trailhead. There will be a sign just to the right near the kiosk indicating Wet Bottom Trail and pointing to Cooper Road Trail.

Distance: Sixteen miles

Average Time: Six to seven hours. Longer for groups and slow animals.

Elevation Gained: 1083 ft. (Max. elevation 2333 ft.)

Trail Type: Mixed mountain soil with many rocks and some roots. There are several stream and creek crossings. The route has both wide and single track.

Rider Skill Level: *Moderate* to *Difficult*. Some sections of the trail have many rocks which can cause stumbling. Narrow ledges will be encountered both descending and ascending. After heavy rain, Abrams Creek can be impassable and treacherous.

Horse Effort: *Strenuous*. The trail would be rated moderate, but the length increases the rating. Pacing your horse will be needed.

Trail Precautions: Horses recommended to be shod or wear boots for foot protection. Hikers will be encountered at various points. The low areas on this route produce many biting flies, so you are strongly encouraged to take bug repellent along with you. Use caution crossing Abrams Creek and climbing the bank on the opposite side. There will be a delayed emergency response in case of an accident.

Resources: Water is abundant along the ride.

Nearest Town: Townsend, TN

Fees and Permits: No fees. Must have Coggins test available upon ranger's request.

Sunshine across the cove.

Seasons: Currently open year-round except Christmas. Riding is discouraged, but not closed, during the winter months because of increased chances of trail erosion or damage.

The Ride

This route will travel counterclockwise, allowing for scenic views from Hatcher Mountain Trail and an easier approach into Abrams Creek.

    Proceed from the parking area to the Abrams Falls Trailhead. You will see a trail sign indicating Wet Bottom Trail on the right and pointing to Cooper Road Trail. Go right, and travel down Wet Bottom Trail beside the stream until you see where horses cross. There are no markers indicating where to cross, so look for horse tracks leading into the stream and on the opposite side. It's a short distance away from where you started, and if you go past where you cross the stream, the trail will become narrow and thick with brush.

Cross the stream, and continue traveling until you reach the first trail intersection. At this intersection, turn right onto a wide gravel path which will lead you by the Elijah Oliver place. Once you pass the old barn on the left, you'll cross a stream and soon arrive at the second trail intersection. Turn left at this intersection, and go the remainder of the .2 miles on Wet Bottom Trail.

At the third intersection, go left, which will be Cooper Road Trail. The sign will indicate Beard Cane Trail is 5.5 miles away. Cooper Road Trail will be wide, coursing through rolling ridges. The forest will be open woods with abundant laurel slicks. Reminisce while you travel here as this section was once an old Native American path, which later became the route for early settlers entering the Cove. Merchandise and goods were hauled in on this route for many years.

One of the many views from Hatcher Mountain Trail.

Abrams Creek Crossing.

After traveling the long distance down Cooper Road, you will come to a four-way intersection. The sign will indicate Little Bottoms Trail is 2.6 miles and is pointing to the left. Go left, traveling on Hatcher Mountain Trail. The views from Hatcher Mountain will be admirable most of the length and make this ride very inspiring. As you near the end of Hatcher Mountain Trail, Abrams Creek can be heard, revealing itself down in the bottom the closer you get.

At the sixth intersection, you will be at Abrams Creek. Horses are not allowed to go left, which would take you to Abrams Falls. Turn right, and immediately begin crossing the creek. Use caution if the water level is high from recent rain. Also, be careful climbing the bank on the opposite side because the ledge is a sheer drop. Travel for another 1.9 miles. Note: Abrams Creek makes a great place to take a long break and is just past the halfway point.

Once you reach the seventh and last trail intersection, turn left, traveling on Rabbit Creek Trail. Portions of this trail are very rocky.

About a mile in from the last intersection, you will cross Rabbit Creek. Campsite 15 for hikers will be up the hill on the right. From this point, the remainder of the trail will be mostly uphill. Nearing the end of Rabbit Creek Trail, you will begin descending until you reach the Abrams Falls Trailhead. The loop will now be complete.

GREGORY BALD TRAIL
Sheep Pen Gap   4.0
Gregory Bald   4.5

TRAIL REGULATIONS

GREGORY BALD

Encompassing trails: Gregory Bald

Trail Features: Flame azaleas blooming at the summit within the ten-acre grassy meadow are a sight to behold in June. Among these red azaleas, you will find other colors such as orange, pink, yellow, and even multicolored. Mountain flowers also grow among the azalea shrubs. And if that isn't enough, the open bald atop the high plain gives a magnificent panoramic view of the surrounding mountains not found many places in the southeastern United States. It looks more like something you would see in Montana. The vibrant green carpet of grass flows and waves in the wind while overlooking Cades Cove. Review the cover of this guide to notice the horse's tail suspended in the wind while overlooking the Cove. If you venture here, you will be enraptured by the sights which will leave an indelible mark upon your soul.

Parking and Trailhead Location: From Townsend, TN, turn right onto Laurel Creek Road at the "Y" intersection to Cades Cove. You will travel west over seven miles and arrive at the Cove. Enter the Cove Loop Road and travel to the far side about six to seven miles. Pass the Abrams Falls Trailhead on the right and then the visitor center a short distance away, also on the right. Forge Creek Road will be straight ahead, near the intersection. It is a gated gravel road beside an open field. Proceed down Forge Creek Road just over a mile until you see Parsons Branch Road on the right and is the only gated gravel road branching off.

Caution: Do not go to the end of Forge Creek Road. You cannot turn around with your trailer. If the Parsons Branch Road gate is open, the parking area is four miles in on the right. It is **one-way only** and exits several miles away onto US 129 in North Carolina, about two hours from Townsend. **Always check with park service before visiting this trail due to access issues**.

Need to Know Information: You'll find this trail located within Cades Cove near the halfway point of the eleven-mile loop road.

Cades Cove Loop Road is closed for bicycle and foot traffic every Saturday and Wednesday morning until 10 a.m. from early May until late September. Otherwise, the road is open year-round to motor vehicles from sunrise until sunset daily, weather permitting.

Start early to avoid heavy traffic on Laurel Creek and Cades Cove Loop Roads. A two-horse trailer is better for maneuvering on the small, narrow, winding road. Do not attempt towing a large trailer. The gate opens thirty minutes after first light, and there will be a line already forming before it opens. You will need copious amounts of patience before reaching the trailhead, especially if you start later in the day. The road is a one-way/one-lane paved road. It may take over an hour to travel eight miles in slow, stop-and-go traffic. If you decide to exit before reaching the trailhead, you will need to take one of the shortcut roads, either Sparks Lane or Hyatt Lane on the left. To avoid tourists on the loop road, get in line before daylight and exit late in the evening. Gates close at dark.

Forge Creek Road: Open April-December, road conditions permitting. Open dates may change year to year. Check the park's website before committing.

Caution: Because of the remote area and limited access, this trail can cause very delayed emergency response for both you and your horse. No one will get to you soon. Likewise, if your truck breaks down anywhere within the Cove, you will have a long wait before help arrives.

Gregory Bald Trail has one horse primitive camp near the Bald, which is campsite 13. You will need to call 865-436-1297 to obtain a backcountry permit.

Begin: Travel from the small parking lot across the road to Gregory Bald Trail. Hannah Mountain Trail will also be at this location.

Narrow section of Gregory Bald Trail.

Blooms on Gregory Bald Trail.

Distance: 8.8 miles.

Average Time: Five to six hours. Longer for groups or slow animals.

Elevation Gain: 2,270 ft. (Max. elevation 4876 ft.)

Rider Skill Level: *Moderate*. The trail is a narrow path on a steady mild incline with a few narrow ledges. Coaching a lesser-skilled rider on this route can be achieved with a well-mannered, experienced horse.

Horse Effort: *Moderate* to *strenuous*. Sturdy, healthy horses are desirable because of the long incline and the overall gain in altitude. Pacing your horse may be required.

Trail Precautions: Horses recommended to be shod or have boots for protection. Hikers will be encountered at various points, usually at the Bald. Roots and rocks can cause stumbling. This trail is notorious for hitting a knee. There will be a delayed emergency response in case of an accident.

Resources: Water is found along the ride and so is grass at Gregory Bald for your horse. Camping is available at Backcountry Campsite 13 Sheep Pen Gap.

Trail Type: Mixed mountain soil with rocks and roots. There are several wet crossings. Mostly narrow single track.

Nearest Town: Townsend, TN

Fees and Permits: No fees. Must have Coggins test available upon ranger's request.

Seasons: Currently open year-round except Christmas. Riding is discouraged, but not closed, during the winter months because of increased chances of trail erosion or damage.

Forge Creek Road: Open April-December, road conditions permitting. Open dates may change year to year. Parsons Branch Road is

almost always closed. Check the park's website before committing, or call the backcountry ranger for questions.

The Ride

This route is not a loop trail, and the hallmark of this ride is at the grassy bald.

Proceed from the parking lot across from the trailhead, and immediately begin ascending at a mild grade for 4.1 miles. The trail will seem to follow up a large gulf most of the way, with water flowing down in the bottom. Shrubs will be along this path and will produce some nice flowery blooms during the summer. Large trees will be growing higher up. There are some decent views across the gulf through the tree line as you ascend.

Around three miles up, you will reach Panther Gap. As you press farther, the trail will become less of a grade nearing the campsites. They will be noticeable on the right of the trail at Sheep Pen Gap in an open flat area. Just beyond the campsites will be Wolf Ridge Trail intersection. Turn left at this junction, and you will reach Gregory Bald in about one-third of a mile. Before reaching the meadow, you will notice the grassy area becoming larger and populated with azalea shrubs. Prepare for a spectacular view and not wanting to leave.

Gregory Bald—a carpet of grass and beautiful scenery.

HORSE CAMPING AT THE COVE

Directions: Go through Townsend, TN on Highway 321 and make a right onto Laurel Creek Road at the Townsend Wye. Follow the signs to Cades Cove. Laurel Creek Road dead-ends at the Cove entrance. Turn left just before entering the Cades Cove Loop Road, and immediately turn left again into the day picnic area. Travel on the one-way road until you reach the gate for the horse camp at the far end. It will be closed but not locked. Open and proceed farther until you reach the camping area. Don't forget to close the gate.

Caution: The day picnic area will be difficult to drive through with a large horse trailer when tourists are occupying the sites. Best to get there early in the morning or late in the evening to avoid these lively visitors. A gooseneck three-horse slant-load trailer is about the maximum size to bring to the camp (twenty-four feet) for maneuvering purposes.

Anthony Creek Horse Camp is the only available area the park provides to stay with your horses near Cades Cove. However, there are four other remote sites found in the backcountry for horse camping within or near the Cove. They are Campsite 3 at Hesse Creek, Campsite 5 on Rich Mountain, Campsite 28 on Lynn Camp Prong, and Campsite 13 at Sheep Pen Gap. A permit should be obtained for the primitive campsites if you plan on staying there.

Anthony Creek has three available spaces, and reservations must be made prior to your arrival. The camp is small but has a vault toilet, picnic

Corrals at Anthony Creek Horse Camp.

tables, fire ring, and three, four-horse open metal stalls. It's not uncommon to hear bears at night in the camp and find paw prints on your truck or trailer. Don't worry, your horses should be fine as there has never been an attack involving horses while corralled. Just make sure you put away all food and garbage sources as the park specifies. Bears will eat horse feed too.

Anthony Creek Trail access runs right in the center of the small camp, and hikers will be passing through. Not sure why park officials designed it this way, so just be aware of non-horse people near your horses. My experience has been that many are friendly and stop to say hello without walking up to the horses. Some may even ask for a picture with them. Whichever is the case, there can be a child or a young person who runs over in their excitement, provoking your horse. Day horse riders may also ride through and cause excitement with your horses. Review the *Local City and Resources* page at the back of this guide for other places to stay with your horses near Cades Cove.

Horse Camp Information and Regulations

Regulations for the Anthony Creek Horse Camp are not provided because they change without notification. Also, all drive-up horse camps in the GSMNP currently operate on the reservation system. You will need to visit www.recreation. gov or call 1-877-444-6777 to reserve a site up to six months in advance. Park officials can answer your questions, but many of your questions can be answered on the park's website. There are additional regulations posted at the campsite you must follow.

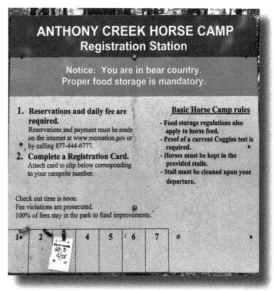

Anthony Creek Horse Camp registration station.

General Codes, Rules and Policies

There are sixty-one national parks found within the United States. Do not assume horseback riding is the same at every federal park because each park has its own set of policies for many reasons, even though they are all federally regulated. It is your sole responsibility to be fully aware of the park's regulations before setting out on the trails. Failure to review or uphold the regulations can result in costly citations, or worse, possible closure of trails for all horseback riding. Some infractions may even include jail time.

In addition, the policies regulating horseback riding can suddenly change without notice, and the park could immediately close for unforeseen reasons. Therefore, it is vital to check the park's website prior to arriving or call the backcountry number where you can speak to a ranger. Phone numbers are provided at the end of this book for your convenience. You can also obtain horseback riding policies at the ranger station in Cades Cove.

The following are general rules and regulations taken from the park's literature at the time of the publication of this book. It is not a comprehensive list, and they have been added to provide an idea of what to expect.

Caution: Do not rely on this guide to inform you of every policy or regulation because it has not been authorized as the defining source. Always contact park officials or review the website prior to your visit.

- Have in hand an up-to-date, original copy of a negative Coggins test for each horse brought into the park

- No pets are allowed on trails in the backcountry

- Stay on designated trails. Know which trails are open to horses by checking with park rangers or the website

- Observe wildlife from a distance, and do not attempt to feed or push them

- Keep horses away from springs

- Do not pick, dig, or remove any plant, flower, or natural object

- Use processed feed instead of whole-grain to eliminate introducing seeds into the park

- Food, drinks, and the equipment to prepare meals are to be kept sealed and out of reach of bears. This includes horse feed

- Garbage must be kept away from bears or disposed of properly

- If camping with horses at backcountry sites, you must use the provided hitching post or use a highline

- If camping at a drive-up horse camp, you must use the corral provided

🐎 All drive-up horse camps operate on a reservation system which requires you to call beforehand

🐎 All backcountry horse campsites require a permit

🐎 Do not take shortcuts or ride cross-country

🐎 Dismount and walk horses across roads or paved areas

🐎 Littering is strictly prohibited

🐎 The park discourages riding your horse from early December until May because of increased wear on the trails and the seasonal trail maintenance program

🐎 The five drive-up horse camps are open through the months of April and October

Emergency Contacts and Info

Below are emergency contacts you may want to save to your cellular device. Call the locations you're planning on riding ahead of time to obtain up-to-date information because there is no cell phone reception in many of the places in the GSMNP. The many peaks, valleys, and remote areas block or hinder radio signals. Sometimes signals can be acquired at higher elevations, but it's not guaranteed. Plan well, and always tell someone your planned destinations and when to expect you back.

🐎 911 — for all emergencies

🐎 865-273-5000 — Blount County Sheriff Department (non-emergency)

🐎 865-436-1294 – Smoky MT Dispatch (emergency)

🐎 865-436-1297 — Smoky MT Backcountry Rangers

🐎 865-436-7318 — Cades Cove Welcoming Center

🐎 865-448-4103 — Anthony Creek Horse Camp

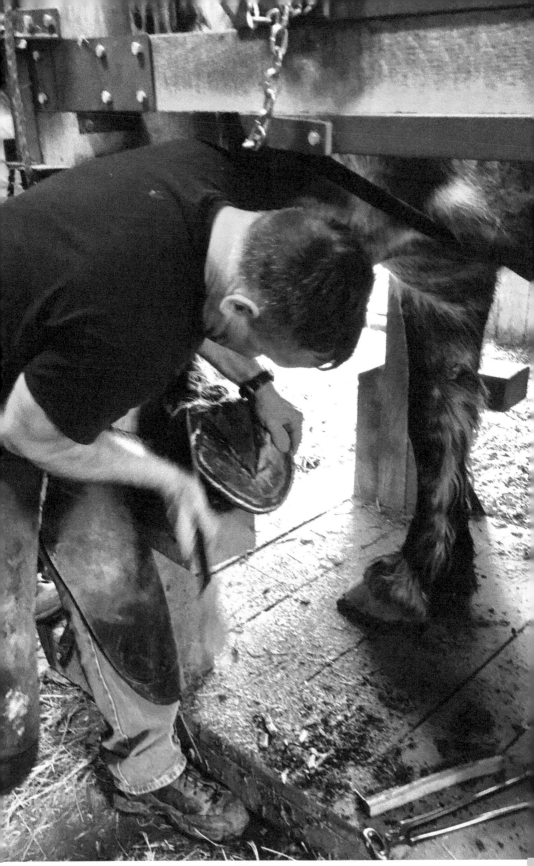

Barefoot Trim on a heavy Draft Horse.

SHOD VS BAREFOOT

THE VALUE OF THE HOOF

The old saying "No foot, no horse" is a true one because anyone who has owned horses has some understanding that horses' feet need regular care. Even though a horse's foot is built rugged and tough, man has subjected horses to greater workloads than they would otherwise experience out in the wild. So, this subject has been added to provide insight into a heavily debated subject in America among those who keep horses. It goes with the territory, much like keeping our automobiles lubed and tuned-up. After all, you will be experiencing the rugged trails within this guide. I bet you have discussed this subject with a farrier and other horse folks once or twice.

In simple terms, many theories and studies have been performed to gain insight into whether horses should go barefoot or shod. There are many factors to consider, and people are on both sides of the fence in our modern times. As a working farrier, I have my own opinion, but I would rather introduce you to some history to help you form your own thoughts on the subject instead of my sharing a lot of boring technical data.

We will separate these folks into two groups. One side believes horses should never be shod with metal shoes and should be kept natural. They profess that if maintained correctly by hoof trimming and diet, a horse can

_99_

participate on any kind of terrain and remain sound while barefoot. Further still, some even proclaim that shoeing is inhumane because of driving a nail through the hoof wall. The other crowd says shoeing is necessary and needed to protect the horse's foot. They claim it is inhumane if you don't give the horse's foot protection.

So, let's take a look back in time and review how horses and man have evolved together. Perhaps we'll discover their thoughts on this subject, helping you to gain a better perspective. I think you will find it very interesting.

Steel shoe with frog support half-pad.

BRIEF HISTORY OF MAN AND EQUINE

Many historians agree that equids were most likely hunted and utilized as food in the earliest of times, but we cannot be sure of this. There's no documentation of whether man and horse forged companion bonds first as we do with our animals today. It is my opinion that both occurred simultaneously.

The exact timeframe when man first tamed horses is not known, but experts have estimated the period to be around 5,500 to 6,000 years ago. Newly discovered evidence has led to the current hypothesis that the Botai culture in the Eurasian Steppes region was the first to domesticate the equids. Regardless of when, as humankind began to farm and establish semi-permanent settlements, some intelligent person realized horses could be tamed, trained, and used to make life easier. There are many ancient artifacts and texts preserved from antiquity to show this correlation. With all the interesting literature that exists on the subject, we don't have to look very far to find proof.

One of the oldest known depictions of equine utilization is dated to 2,800 BC. An ancient Sumerian art piece depicts a war cart being pulled by a pair of asses. Yet another well-preserved artifact from Egypt, dated somewhere around 1,500 BC, clearly represents a pair of elaborately decorated horses pulling a chariot. Sumerians, like Egyptians, appear to have also been advanced horse cultures too.

Egyptians were no doubt excellent horsemen and very good at recordkeeping, which provided modern humans examples of how they kept and utilized horses. Their horses received excellent care and lived in fine stables, living far better than most people in that era.

Romans were similar in the ways they used and kept horses. Horses were considered a sign of royalty and wealth, and some were even worshiped. They used them in ceremonies, hunting, war, and probably anywhere else they were found fitting. It is an understatement to say that when humans first discovered the value of the horse, lives were changed forever. Humans found new roles for horses, expanding their jobs from farming land to participating in ancient games, using them in wars, and finally, riding them for pleasure.

As civilizations prospered and cultures perfected their craft, training horses became a highly sought after trade, and owning them became a status symbol. From kings and other wealthy men down to the common person, people needed their horses to perform everyday tasks. One specific soldier who lived in ancient times is held in high esteem for his skills in keeping and training horses. In fact, his insight was so brilliant, his work, written over 2,400 years ago, is still reflected upon today.

The Athenian warrior Xenophon wrote a text called "The Art of Horsemanship." In it, he discusses training, care, and selection of military horses. His writings are regarded as the first to detail fundamentals for dressage and natural horsemanship. Even today, we can gain a lot of knowledge from Xenophon's wisdom. Of course, there are other excellent horsemen found throughout history we can learn from also.

Historical records indicate cultures that mastered horsemanship became supreme by conquering other settlements through overtaking their lands and therefore increasing their overall reach. This, no doubt, made the horse even more valuable to our ancestors, for it provided the mechanization for warfare. Horses were used extensively for transport, shock tactics, and battle charges. Today's culture owes much of what we know about horses to these ancient civilizations in their race to conquer, because many innovations are heavily credited to them in training, development of equipment, and origination of specific breeds.

Well-known cultures that utilized horses:

- The Egyptians used horses to pull chariots as early as 3000 BC. Their battle tactics were very successful, helping them to become a great nation.

- The Roman Empire used horses extensively to rule and conquer. Their tactics and training were highly sought after in ancient times.

- The Greeks, specifically Alexander the Great (350 BC), conquered Asia on horseback. He tamed his famous war-horse at age ten. Alexander named his powerful horse Bucephalus, which translates to Ox-head. The famed horse then carried him into many victorious battles and then fatefully succumbed to wounds at the battle of Hydaspes.

- China (Qin Dynasty 211-206 BC): The emperor of this era was buried with full-size terra-cotta statues of his cavalry to protect him in death. Perfectly detailed warriors, horses, and chariots have been well preserved to illustrate the significance of horses in warfare.

- Genghis Khan Dynasty: Genghis Khan could not have conquered and ruled the largest land empire in world history without Mongolian ponies and use of rawhide coverings to protect their hooves.

- Medieval period fifth to sixteenth century AD: Heavily armored knights with their horses were powerful and dreaded. They carried out warfare on behalf of those to whom their allegiance belonged on heavy built and armored horses.

- The American Civil War: Several million horses were used by both sides of the American armies. The total number of horses and mules killed in the Civil War is estimated to be more than one million.

🐎 World War I: Millions of horses, ponies, and mules were used. It is estimated that over eight million were killed. Because of the vulnerability of horses to modern machine gun and artillery fire, horses finally were replaced with machinery, reducing their numbers significantly in warfare.

A Biblical text written around the sixth century BC depicts a war-horse. God himself is talking to Job.

> ¹⁹ *"Have you given the horse strength?*
> *Have you clothed his neck with thunder?*
> ²⁰ *Can you frighten him like a locust?*
> *His majestic snorting strikes terror.*
> ²¹ *He paws in the valley, and rejoices in his strength;*
> *He gallops into the clash of arms.*
> ²² *He mocks at fear, and is not frightened;*
> *Nor does he turn back from the sword.*
> ²³ *The quiver rattles against him,*
> *The glittering spear and javelin.*
> ²⁴ *He devours the distance with fierceness and rage;*
> *Nor does he come to a halt because the trumpet has sounded.*
> ²⁵ *At the blast of the trumpet he says, 'Aha!'*
> *He smells the battle from afar,*
> *The thunder of captains and shouting*

> —*New King James Version (NKJV)*
> *Job 39:19-25*

Sports

Horses have been used extensively in many other areas throughout history, not just in the savageries of war. Equestrian sports were also a big part of the lives of horsemen in ancient times. Polo is an example of such a sport in the sixth century BC. The nomadic Persian and Chinese civilizations played polo some 2,000 years ago. Another ancient sport called Buzkashi was played in Central Asia, dating back to the Genghis Khan era. Moving forward a few centuries, we see many depictions of jousting in the later medieval period. Modern times provide us with flat racing, rodeo, show jumping, dressage, and more.

Western Horses

1. Western pleasure
2. Working cow horse
3. Cutting
4. Halter
5. Rodeo – Barrel racing, bulldogging, calf roping, and team penning

English Horses

1. Eventing
2. Dressage
3. Show jumping
4. Hunt seat
5. Fox hunting
6. American Saddlebred shows
7. Polo

Flat Racing

1. Endurance
2. Harness racing
3. Quarter horse racing: 330 to 880 yards
4. Thoroughbred racing: 4 furlongs to 1¾ miles

Other Types

1. Steeplechase
2. Native Indian Racing
3. Others

If my intuition serves me well, I believe man first tamed the horse, then used it as a beast of burden for chores, such as tilling the ground for crops, moving heavy objects, and then pulling carts and buggies. In those early days, man needed help transporting large items and containers of goods. Moving possessions on the back of the animal wherever tribes migrated seems logical, thereby relieving man of the many associated burdens. This, in turn, helped people to wander farther in search of better areas in which to thrive. The phrase, "A dog may be man's best friend…but the horse wrote history," is a true one.

It goes without saying that keeping equids requires giving them ample care and attention. After all, they are put to extraordinary use by humankind. I cannot think of any other animal man has used so extensively for his pleasure and endeavors, whether for good or evil.

Likewise, I hope you are now beginning to see the importance of the evolution of the farrier trade and why it was so important and necessary. Keeping the horse sound on his feet is as important today as it was in ancient times, when people relied much more heavily on their horses simply to survive. This book would not be complete without the farrier's role and how this craft evolved throughout history alongside the horse. So, let's take a quick look at the farrier trade.

Benjamin Franklin was credited for the famous quote below. I think it ends this chapter well and transitions to the next chapter.

> *"For the want of a nail the shoe was lost,*
> *For the want of a shoe the horse was lost,*
> *For the want of a horse the rider was lost,*
> *For the want of a rider the battle was lost,*
> *For the want of a battle the kingdom was lost,*
> *And all for the want of a horseshoe-nail."*

The Blacksmith and Farrier Trade

The modern definition of the word farrier is "a craftsman who trims and shoes horses." But this Anglo-French word ultimately can be traced back to the Latin word *ferrum,* meaning "iron" or "one who works with iron." The earliest known blacksmith is found in Biblical text. In Genesis 4:22, we find a man by the name of Tubal-Cain who forged different types of metal. However, there is no mention of horses or the practice of shoeing them.

Though, sometime in early history, ancient people recognized the importance of protecting their horses' feet from wear and tear. The

Nailing a modern Keg shoe to a front foot.

earliest known protective covering appears to have originated from Asia. These crafty people wrapped their horses' hooves in woven grass sandals for protection, while neighboring people used similar materials for the same purpose. It is believed that these ancient methods are still used today in some less-developed areas of the world. Soon, tougher materials were sought by craftsmen who were looking for a better solution. Evidence concludes that rawhide was the next material extensively utilized by the ancient civilizations.

The Egyptians, Romans, and Greeks were some of the well-known cultures experimenting with animal hides as hoof protection. As those cultures

Mules need TLC too. The common belief that mules can go without shoes is a misconception. Mule's feet are typically smaller and need hoof protection the same as horses.

progressed with their use of leather, some specimens found in excavation sites had metal studs fixed to the bottom for added protection and traction. Experiments by these cultures to protect the horse's foot most likely encouraged nearby people to attempt better techniques, each group building off the knowledge of another.

As we look ahead in time, we can see the Mongolians are credited for perfecting the technique of affixing rawhide to the horse's foot. Their wide geographical range of conquering proves the effectiveness of their practice. In addition, historians have located and retrieved leather shoes from antiquities, but evidence has been found which shows some cultures used full metal shoes during the same time leather was utilized. With our ability to look back over time, we can now see ancient cultures advancing to something akin to the modern metal horseshoe.

Currently, the Celts and Gauls are credited for being the first civilizations to have nailed a metal shoe to a horse's foot. Their custom of burying horses with their masters preserved the artifacts that archaeologists can now study. The initial relic appeared in Europe, dating around the first century BC, when a horseshoe, complete with nails, was found in the tomb of a Frankish king in Belgium. Further, the Gauls and Celts are reported to have had superior cavalry units, even before the early Roman armies.

Some would argue it was the Chinese or the Romans who first nailed a metal shoe to a horse's foot. Regardless of whoever was the first to do so, artifacts are still being found which reveal that ancient cultures knew the importance of protecting the horse's foot.

The thoroughbred racehorse "Popcorn Delight," who also was used in the filming of Seabiscuit, a movie released in 2003.

Modern Era

If ancient people recognized the need and importance for protecting the equine foot, it only stands to reason that modern civilization should have a deeper understanding because of the artifacts and literature found. Also, I don't think our ancestors would bother with going to such great lengths to protect the foot if it were not needed.

My instructor while I was in farrier school tried to illustrate how the natural bare foot holds up when put to work, even if it's not a hoof. It went something like this—a wealthy explorer sought to go on a long expedition in Africa. He hired many of the local natives to carry his equipment and personal belongings. About fifty miles into the journey, the natives' feet became sore and injured from carrying the equipment over the rough terrain. Thus, the expedition had to be abandoned because of the wear and tear on the natives' bare feet. The moral of the story represents that humans, just like animals, need

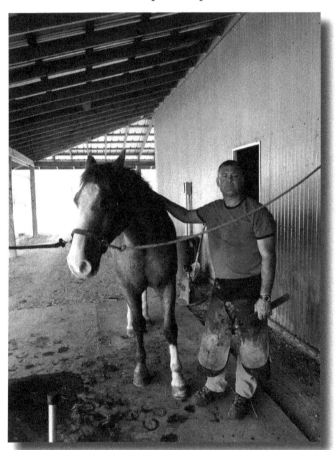

Finishing up with the Appaloosa horse "Blade." Used in many episodes of the Walking Dead TV Series and commercials. Andrew Lincoln, character name Rick Grimes, rode this horse.

foot protection at times of work, even though they have tough natural feet. History reveals it, and there is no disputing it.

But does this still mean every horse must be shod for protection? The answer is no. Even though we understand horses need foot protection, there are other factors that help us determine the need. Those factors are: type of horse, genetics, health, workload, and the environment in which it lives. Every situation and horse must be evaluated carefully. Horses in drier climates tend to have tougher feet and can tolerate going barefoot better than those in the wetter climates. Moisture softens the hoof, making it more vulnerable to wear, and there is always a higher chance of bacteria thriving in wet climates.

While I was working one day, a young lady asked if I would trim her horse. I took the offer but questioned her about how she would be utilizing her horse. She replied by telling me her plans were to barrel race and do some trail riding. While recommending putting metal shoes on her horse, I could see the agitation welling up in her. The blonde proclaimed, no joke intended, "It's not natural or humane to put nails in the hoof." She further lectured me on barefoot trims, as if I didn't know anything about my trade. I replied, "Then why do you have piercings in your ears, nose, and mouth, and why do you wear shoes? Are those tattoos on your arm too?" The deer in the headlights look soon gripped her face as if she had never thought of those aspects. I further explained that horses had no pain where the nail penetrated the hardened, keratinized hoof wall.

Further, when horses tear and chip their bare feet from use, bacteria and fungus can easily invade those small cracks and begin to eat live tissue, resulting in weak, diseased, and painful feet. There are alternatives in the shoe department, but neglecting to protect your horse's foot is inhumane when you put him to work. After presenting several options to her for many shoeing techniques, she relented and I shod her horse.

Consider that horses stand twenty-three hours per day on average. Their large body cannot tolerate lying down for prolonged periods because they are at risk for pressure sores and other problems as adults. The horse has a mechanical feature in the leg called the stay apparatus which locks the legs and allows them to stand while sleeping. Therefore, they need their feet more so than other animals to survive.

Shoes are an essential component for protecting the feet of horses and mules used on long rides in rugged mountains. Horseshoes are not only for protection; they also serve as traction on slippery ground. Additionally, devices can be added to metal shoes for traction on slick rocks as well.

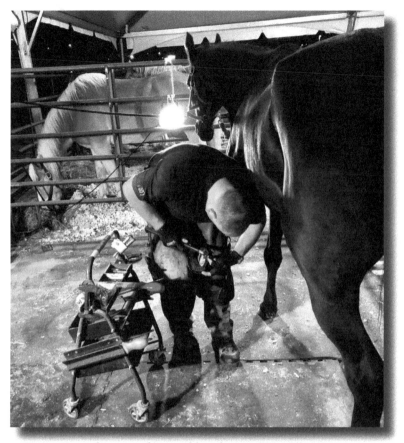

Downtown Atlanta applying rubber shoes to "Magic" at 3 a.m.
For filming scenes of Season Nine of the Walking Dead TV Series.
Khary Payton, character name King Ezekiel, rode this horse.

Another crucial aspect of applying horseshoes is for therapeutic reasons, helping the horse with lameness issues.

If nailing a shoe on is still not your cup of tea, there are other alternatives. Rubber boots have become more popular over the last decade as technology has advanced. They work well in some environments, but don't think you will save money bypassing the farrier. You still have to trim the hoof and fit the boot properly. They are pricey and may come off in deep mud and extremely rocky terrain. If you lose one, you will have to purchase another. You'll get about a year's worth of use out of boots when used regularly.

Still, there are other options, such as gluing on shoes. You can even build a plastic shoe by using resins from manufacturers like Vettec or Equilox. When applied, they instantly set and harden, forming a tough covering over the hoof.

Again, these alternatives are pricey compared to the old method of nailing on a metal shoe.

Perhaps you are beginning to see the importance of protecting your horse's feet and the many options available to modern-day horse owners. One important aspect I should mention—anything you apply to the foot can cause changes to the hoof capsule. Sometimes, if done incorrectly, damage can occur up to and including permanent lameness. Also, horses shod most of their lives can acquire contracted feet over time. Having said that, I will remind you again, you must carefully evaluate every situation, taking into account the type of horse, genetics, health, workload, and the environment in which it lives. Choosing what is best suited for your animal is vitally important. There are many options for your horse or mule; I only ask that you care for your animal's feet by hiring a competent well-trained farrier. Your horse is worth it.

The pictures throughout the text are examples of some horses I've had the privilege of working with while performing my trade. Still, there are many I work with that are no less important.

Hot shoeing kills bacteria, forms a tough barrier by cauterization and creates the tightest possible fit-up shoe to hoof.

LOCAL CITIES, RESOURCES, AND CONTACTS

Townsend, TN is one of the three gateways to the park and is the closest town to Cades Cove at seven miles. It is often referred to as the peaceful side of the Smokies. This small town offers attractions such as bike riding, fishing, camping, rafting, and swimming. Still, there are other activities to find within this quiet scenic area, such as the Tremont Institute. Tuckalechee Caverns and a history museum are nearby also. Be sure to stop by the Smoky Mountain Visitor Center to find information about the park and surrounding area.

In addition, there are private stables located in Townsend if you're bringing your horse to ride the nearby trails at the Cove. Gilbertson's Lazy Horse Retreat is great and has some really nice cabins for couples. Melody, the owner, also provides other options upon request and availability. I highly recommend contacting her for reservations.

If you're looking for some entertainment within the main tourist areas after riding and stabling your horse, Pigeon Forge is an easy drive only eighteen miles away and Gatlinburg is twenty-five miles away. Dollywood, a popular theme park, is located in Pigeon Forge. There are plenty of restaurants and stores to fill your every need.

Nearest Feed Store to Townsend
Tractor Supply
1800 W Lamar Alexander Pkwy
Maryville, TN 37801
865-681-3336

Ag Central Farmers' Cooperative
1514 W Broadway Ave
Townsend TN, 37801
865-982-2761

Horse Boarding, Camping, and Cabin Rentals for Horsemen near Cades Cove

Below are two retreats offering riders a place to stay and ride at the Cove. Both have ride-out access into the Cove from the stable. Review their website and give them a call.

🐎 Lazy Horse Retreat
938 Schoolhouse Gap Road
Townsend, TN 37882
Phone: 865-448-6810

Email: lazyhrse@comcast.net
Website: lazyhorseretreat.com

🐎 Orchard Cove Stables
1263 Schoolhouse Gap Road
Townsend, TN 37882

Phone:423-400-6667
Email: orhardcovestables@yahoo.com
Website: www.orchardcovestables.com

Horses stabled at Melody Gilbertson's Lazy Horse Retreat.

PRESERVATION FOR THE GREAT SMOKY MOUNTAINS HORSE TRAILS

I t is my sincere hope this guide book will inspire fellow equestrians to preserve and enjoy the treasures the Great Smoky Mountain National Park offers. To that end, I've partnered with the Friends of the Smokies to create a way for equestrians to assist in funding horse trail maintenance and continued preservation in the Great Smoky Mountains. This park does not charge entry fees, unlike many other national parks, so they partially rely on help from outside sources to raise public awareness. Friends of the Smokies is a nonprofit organization dedicated to historic preservation, wildlife management, and environmental education for the park. With the publication of this book, they are adding a new fund specifically for the horseback riders who love riding here.

No donation amount is too great or too small. Will you contribute to this worthwhile campaign so that we can keep these trails open and updated for future generations?

Hey, send charitable donations to:
Friends of the Smokies
Leave No Trace: Equestrian Fund
PO Box 1660
Kodak, TN 37764-7660

ABOUT THE AUTHOR AND HORSE

Jody L. Burrage, an avid mountain rider, continues to work as a blacksmith and farrier in his community and has provided his services for several movie horses and other remarkable steeds. As an experienced horseman, he has attained many valuable credentials, helping him to craft this guide. Among his contributions working with equines and horse trail preservation groups, he previously served as a nationally registered paramedic, firefighter, and rescue technician. He has further experiences in the outdoors, such as hunting, fishing, rock-climbing, rappelling, and caving. As if those weren't enough, he enjoys the sport of open water diving in the ocean and more.

The extraordinary horse utilized in the creation of this guide, providing the front-row seat on the beautiful trails, is a sixteen-hand, 1300-pound, eight-year-old Spotted Saddle Horse named Heavy D. Whether carrying his owner with comfort, fording streams and rivers, powering up rugged mountains, or galloping down trails, he always has remained a steady and faithful companion.

Jody L. Burrage and Heavy D.

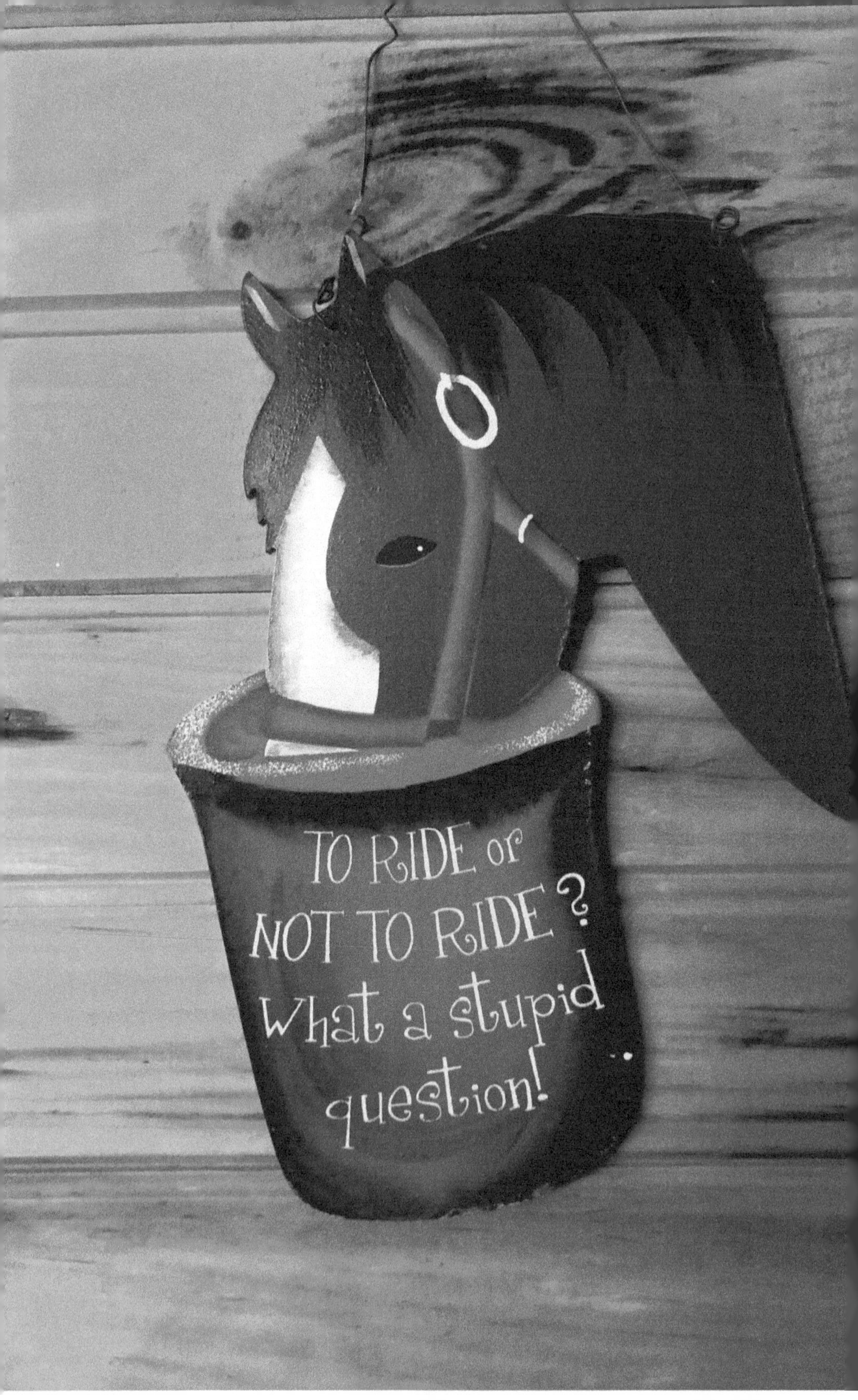
TO RIDE or
NOT TO RIDE?
What a stupid
question!

BIBLIOGRAPHY

Bledsoe. Porter. Cherry. "Essentials of Paramedic Care" Pearson Prentice Hall. Upper Saddle River, NJ

Butler, Doug. "The Principles of Horseshoeing" Doug Butler Publisher. Maryville, MO

Colles, Chris. Ware, Ron "The Principles of Farriery" J.A. Allen London, Eng

Franklin D. Roosevelt Presidential Library and Museum. General Facts & Figures. (https://www.fdrlibrary.org/fdr-facts)

Harris, Moira. Swinney, Nicole. "Horses" Metro Books New York, NY

Johnson, Deb. Welcome to Helpful Horse Hints. Cherokee Indians and Horses. (http://horsehints.org/IndianCherokee.htm)

Library of Congress. Franklin D. Roosevelt. Reproduction Number: LC-DIG-npcc-01391 (digital file from original) (https://www.loc.gov/pictures/item/2016827746/)

Molen van Ee, Patricia. Library of Congress. Maps of the Great Smoky Mountains National Park. (https://www.loc.gov/collections/national-parks-maps/articles-and-essays/maps-of-great-smoky-mountains-national-park/)

National Park Foundation. Ancient Mountains, Ancient Wonders. Great Smoky Mountains National Park. (https://www.nationalparks.org/explore-parks/great-smoky-mountains-national-park)

National Park Service. Great Smoky Mountains Blooming Shrubs. 2016, July 11. (https://www.nps.gov/grsm/learn/nature/blooming-shrubs.htm)

National Park Service. Great Smoky Mountains Weather. (https://www.nps.gov/grsm/planyourvisit/weather.htm)

Parker, Amber. Forests of the Great Smoky Mountains National Park. (2009. Forests of GSMNP.doc) (http://gsmit.org/wp-content/uploads/2017/10/forests-of-the-smokies.pdf)

Smithsonian. Franklin D. Roosevelt, 1882-1945. (https://www.si.edu/spotlight/
    highlights-franklin-d-roosevelt-1882-1945)

Visit My Smokies. (https://www.visitmysmokies.com/area-information/smoky-
    mountains/)

Wolff, Emily. 7 Basic Facts About the Smoky Mountains That Might Surprise You.
    (https://www.visitmysmokies.com/blog/smoky-mountains/basic-facts-about-
    smoky-mountains/) 2015, April10.